PRAISE FOR *share*

"This beautiful cookbook offers not only insightful, delicious, seasonal recipes, but also a window into a wonderful organization, FoodShare. Each recipe shares not just amounts, ingredients, and techniques but also the joy and love of cooking that is the soul of the kitchen—whether in a home or in a restaurant!"
AARON JOSEPH BEAR ROBE, CHEF/OWNER, KERIWA CAFE

"A book you can not only read, but actually cook with— giving you more reasons to garden, shop locally and sustainably, and share a home-cooked meal with family and friends."
WAYNE ROBERTS, WRITER AND FOOD POLICY ANALYST

"A much-needed and practical resource for healing our broken food system. FoodShare's ability to involve its friends, young and old, in this growing 'Good Food Revolution' is critical to the success of efforts to make nutritious and affordable food accessible at every level."
WILL ALLEN, AUTHOR OF *The Good Food Revolution*

share

Delicious Dishes *from* FoodShare *and* Friends

ADRIENNE DE FRANCESCO *with* MARION KANE

Foreword by FRANCES MOORE LAPPÉ

Between the Lines
Toronto, Canada

share: Delicious Dishes from FoodShare and Friends
© 2012 FoodShare Toronto

First published in 2012 by
Between the Lines
401 Richmond Street West
Studio 277
Toronto, Ontario M5V 3A8
Canada
1-800-718-7201
www.btlbooks.com

LIBRARY AND ARCHIVES CANADA CATALOGUING IN PUBLICATION
De Francesco, Adrienne
Share : delicious dishes from FoodShare and friends
/ Adrienne De Francesco with Marion Kane.

Includes index.
Issued also in electronic formats.
ISBN 978-1-926662-87-9

1. Cooking. 2. FoodShare Toronto (Organization).
3. Cookbooks. I. Kane, Marion II. Title.

TX714.D398 2012   641.5   C2012-903713-3

Photography by Laura Berman, GreenFuse Photos
Food Testing and Styling by Lesleigh Landry & Katie Compton
Printed in Canada

FoodShare is a proud United Way Toronto member agency.

Between the Lines gratefully acknowledges assistance for its publishing activities from the Canada Council for
the Arts, the Ontario Arts Council, the Government of Ontario through the Ontario Book Publishers Tax Credit
program and through the Ontario Book Initiative, and the Government of Canada through the Canada Book Fund.

For Stuart Coles and Jennifer Welsh, who started the move-ment for FoodShare Toronto and the Toronto Food Policy Council with their vision of a new food system in which everyone has good, healthy food and farming is sustainable. And for cooks everywhere working to build that new, just food system, one delicious home-cooked meal at a time.

Contents

Foreword: FoodShare Toronto, Changing the World

I was delighted to hear that FoodShare Toronto was collecting its best recipes and capturing some of the stories of its inspiring work.

When I wrote *Diet for a Small Planet* in 1971, I challenged the idea that hunger was caused by a shortage of food. In reality, then and now, hunger is caused by a shortage of democracy—by people being denied a voice in meeting their essential needs. Of course I could not have imagined that 41 years later, groups like FoodShare would achieve such success in helping to birth a new and respectful food system that gives people that voice. They are a beautiful exemplar of what I talk about in my new book, *EcoMind: Changing the Way We Think, to Create the World We Want*.

In 1994, I spoke at the FoodShare annual general meeting while I was on a book tour promoting the need for citizen engagement. Then, on the recommendation of executive director Debbie Field, my daughter Anna and I went to Brazil and saw the strikingly positive changes that can happen when officials make food a human right.

Most recently, when I was in Toronto to speak about *EcoMind*, I had the great pleasure of visiting FoodShare on one of its famous Tuesday fresh produce packing days and seeing first hand the excitement of people of all incomes, backgrounds, and ages, standing shoulder to shoulder to build new relations of mutuality. FoodShare was full of hope that day, and full of the smells of home cooking as so many of us—volunteers, guests, staff, youth interns, Grade 7 and 8 students—sat down to an amazing meal of minestrone soup, Kenyan kale, rice, jerk chicken or tofu, coleslaw, FoodShare salad, and apple cake.

On a tour of the food hub that FoodShare has built in the middle of a decommissioned high school, I was struck by the power of Debbie's idea that the school garden is the epicentre of community empowerment, and that by teaching students to cook, compost, and keep bees and chickens—by bringing Food Literacy to schools—we can create the new world we want in the belly of the old, decaying system.

It is far too late and things are far too bad for pessimism, and that is why groups like FoodShare are at the leading edge of the shift from a "scarcity mind" to an "eco-mind," changing the world.

Please keep this book close at hand, celebrate the food movement heroes it profiles, and of course try the recipes, from the magnificently simple strawberry juice, rooted in the history of First Nations peoples, to roasted celery root mash with sautéed mushrooms, kale, and pepper purée, a gourmet vegan dish that will thrill your dinner guests.

But most important, be inspired, as I am, by Debbie and the FoodShare volunteers, who each day put food first in their lives, cooking from scratch, building new partnerships with farmers, advocating for right-to-food public policies, and living the EcoMind food system.

—FRANCES MOORE LAPPÉ

The original food hub in Canada.
SPRING GILLARD,
COMPOST DIARIES BLOG

Good Healthy Food for All

All over the world, food is celebrated as the basis of family, community, health, and life.

At FoodShare, sharing food is central to all that we do: our programs, our organization, and our culture. Walk in any day of the week and the smell of cooking greets you. Staff, volunteers, and guests eat together daily. Arriving visitors are offered fruit, coffee, and tea and we share food over every meeting, most often a "Food-Share plate" of vegetables, fruit, hummus, and a healthy baked treat.

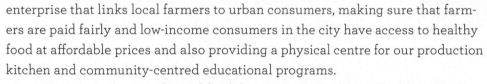

FoodShare Toronto is literally all about food, from organizing school-based student nutrition programs to distributing subsidized Good Food Boxes full of fresh produce from our Field to Table Community Food Hub; from teaching students Food Literacy to leading community kitchens; and from helping start community gardens to teaching new parents how to make baby food from scratch. Our community food hub is a non-profit social enterprise that links local farmers to urban consumers, making sure that farmers are paid fairly and low-income consumers in the city have access to healthy food at affordable prices and also providing a physical centre for our production kitchen and community-centred educational programs.

We aim to make complicated food decisions as simple as possible, providing empowerment through tools, skills, information, and fresh produce and by modelling our own food values in the meals we share every day.

So when Marion Kane, food writer extraordinaire, suggested a cookbook of the best recipes from FoodShare and our friends, we were thrilled. Marion proposed the ideal title, *share*, brought her intuition and expertise from decades as the *Toronto Star*'s food editor, and worked hard alongside a professional recipe tester and our kitchen staff to make sure that each recipe would be perfect every time. Marion, thank you for your inspiration, advice, and much more all along the way.

It was really hard to limit our selection of recipes from the touching bounty of many hundreds submitted from across Canada. A very big thank you to everyone for sending your special recipes, and our apologies that we could not include them all.

Sharing food is such an important personal experience. The smell of my mother's chicken soup always thrilled me as the whole house filled with a warmth that came from the hours it took to cook and from the love my mother, Brenda, would pour into the pot.

My mother's chicken soup (page 55) was central to her cultural identity as a Jewish refugee to the United States who arrived without money or family after the Second World War. It represented her tie to her own parents, their home and background. She never tired of telling stories about the importance of chicken soup in Jewish literature and history, its health benefits, or how many people she could feed with one chicken: soup the first day, schnitzel from the white meat the second, leftover soup eaten down to the bones for days. Chicken soup meant that it was a holiday or a special occasion, so there were many reasons to be excited when that delicious smell was in the air.

Sharing home-cooked meals is also an important part of building a new food system that we hope will be both just and sustainable. Against the dominant fast food and processed food system, many of us around the world are working to create a new culture in which we all slow down enough to cook and eat real food.

FoodShare advocates for policies to ensure adequate incomes so that everyone can afford healthy food and farmers can make a living. We want to change schools to ensure that all students eat at least one healthy meal daily and are taught to cook, garden, compost, and understand food. Our programs provide subsidized fresh produce to make healthy food more accessible in low-income communities and in schools.

And we encourage all people, of all incomes—men and women, young children, teenagers, and seniors—to cook using recipes that are not expensive or complex but that smell, look, and taste delicious.

Whether we are in our own homes or at FoodShare, picking what to eat is complex. How can FoodShare balance opposition to GMO foods (genetically modified organisms) and support for sustainable local food when most of those who buy from us cannot afford organic food? How can we honour our commitment to local farmers and also respect the cultural tastes of immigrants who feel a deep connection with and comfort from home foods, such as mangoes, that are not grown in Canada? In puzzling this out, FoodShare's director of social enterprise Zahra Parvinian, catering co-ordinator Sybil Pinnock, kitchen co-ordinator

Jesús Gomez, and I developed a framework to serve as our guide. We choose delicious, healthy, affordable, culturally appropriate foods and prioritize local and seasonal when feasible, organic when the price is similar to non-organic, and fair trade for imports when available.

This can mean hard choices. We stopped buying sustainably produced beef from Bryan and Cathy Gilvesy at Y U Ranch because it was not halal, although we could afford it and noticed the improved quality and taste. We hope in the future that sustainably produced halal meat will become available, but in the meantime, many who eat at FoodShare will eat only halal.

Honouring cultural diversity means ordering and serving foods that are imported as well as local. Though FoodShare distributes as much food grown in Ontario as possible, we see important cultural and health reasons to include imported food as well. Throughout the book there is a focus on what is grown in this province, but you will also find dishes that use dates or pineapples.

The dishes also highlight a variety of proteins. FoodShare works with many communities and cultures, all of which have favourites and traditions. Our own kitchen develops creative recipes using the full range of proteins from nuts and seeds to grains, beans, and legumes, and from cheese to many kinds of meat and fish. And we also try to make sure that we provide more than one choice daily, so if meat is served a vegan option is also always available. Using proteins that are not derived from animals is important to many of us for health, ethical or environmental reasons, as a money-saving measure, or simply as an exploration of different flavours and textures.

Though this is neither an official guide to healthy eating with documented nutrition information nor a diet book for those who want to lose or gain weight, its recipes will help you follow a healthier diet. At FoodShare we promote eating 8 to 10 servings of fresh vegetables and fruit a day, and this cookbook is filled with recipes to make that easy, from vegetable-rich salads, snacks, mains, and side dishes to many desserts with fruit.

We wanted this book to be filled with recipes that impart the joy and ease of cooking delicious, healthy food and the stories of the people who submitted recipes. And so from all of our kitchens to all of yours, we hope you will enjoy trying these dishes and discover new favourites to share with family and friends. Happy cooking!

—DEBBIE FIELD, EXECUTIVE DIRECTOR, FOODSHARE TORONTO

Preface:
Dishes and Dishing

This book is a celebration of the power of food to bring people together, to nourish both body and soul, and to inspire us. It is also a tribute to how FoodShare Toronto stirs the pot, dishing up heartening stories and easy ways for us all to feel good about saying yes to food.

As in a cherished collection of handwritten recipe cards, each dish you find here is a treasured favourite representing much more. In fact, the process of gathering recipes was as much about discovering all the wonderful ways in which FoodShare connects and supports people in Toronto and across Canada as it was about the food.

We received recipes from the volunteers who help us pack fresh produce and co-ordinate community Good Food Box stops, and from those who run student nutrition programs. Others came from funding partners and individual donors, from teachers and students, from community gardeners, from academics, politicians, and famous chefs, and from community partners and staff. Reading each one was an exploration of our diverse cultural traditions, of the great comfort food provides and, best of all, of sharing.

Each of the hundreds who answered our call responded with a warm anecdote about the meaning of the recipe, always mentioning how they first encountered FoodShare and the place the organization holds in their hearts. We are thankful to you all and only wish we could have included every recipe.

It was fascinating to discover that many are most proud of their desserts and baked goods, and to learn that plums and zucchini have inspired volumes of diverse recipes.

This is a collection like no other, one we hope you will keep close in your kitchen and turn to again and again for recipes you can find nowhere else: Michele Landsberg's latke recipe, the creation of her mother, Lee; Jack Layton's bouillabaisse; chicken soup from Debbie Field's mother; pumpkin leaves in peanut butter sauce with millet sadza from Tinashe Kanengoni; roasted celery root mash with sautéed mushrooms, kale, and pepper purée from Jared Davis, Art Eggleton's favourite Indian-spiced shrimp; Harriet Friedmann's Louisiana gumbo; and many others.

We are proud to include signature recipes from FoodShare's team of chefs Alvin Rebick, Sybil Pinnock, and Jesús Gomez, who have passed along tried and true winners from our daily lunches, their Field to Table Catering company, and FoodShare's healthy high school cafeteria, the Good Food Café. Marion has also contributed many of her favourite dishes, her very best recipes honed to perfection over years.

Every recipe has been thoroughly tested to guarantee ease and success. Fruit and vegetables are assumed to be medium size unless otherwise specified, and should be washed before being prepared. Carrots, parsnips, beets, cucumbers, and potatoes should be scrubbed but not peeled unless specified. Onions, garlic, and shallots are assumed to be peeled unless the recipe indicates otherwise.

Along with FoodShare's kitchen team, we have Lesleigh Landry to thank for dedicating countless hours with Marion to ensuring that the recipes work every time. And recipes were selected only after a unanimous thumbs-up from a rigorous tasting panel that featured, besides the official experts, our toughest critic, Lesleigh's seven-year-old daughter, Mireille.

Even the planning and composition of this book was a privilege, a delicious process in which we shared many hopes and many meals: from vegan Chinese stir fries and mock meats to Indian thalis, Korean hot pots to Lebanese za'atar bread and hearty stewed legumes, and copious amounts of great espresso. Along the way, we got to know one another and exchange our own stories.

Our deep thanks to the many who took the time to share their expertise and recommendations, including the tireless and astute Alison Fryer of The Cookbook Store and her staff; marketing maven Felicia Quon; the wonderful and patient folks at Between the Lines; Laura Berman of GreenFuse Photos, whose camera always best captures FoodShare's work and who is responsible for all the tantalizing photos; our editor, Camilla Blakeley; our designer, Ingrid Paulson, who brought our vision to life on paper; and Stuart Ross of Bull Dog Coffee.

share has already cooked up many new favourites and much joy and hope, and it is our great pleasure to pass it along to you and encourage you to cook, to enjoy, and to share.

salads

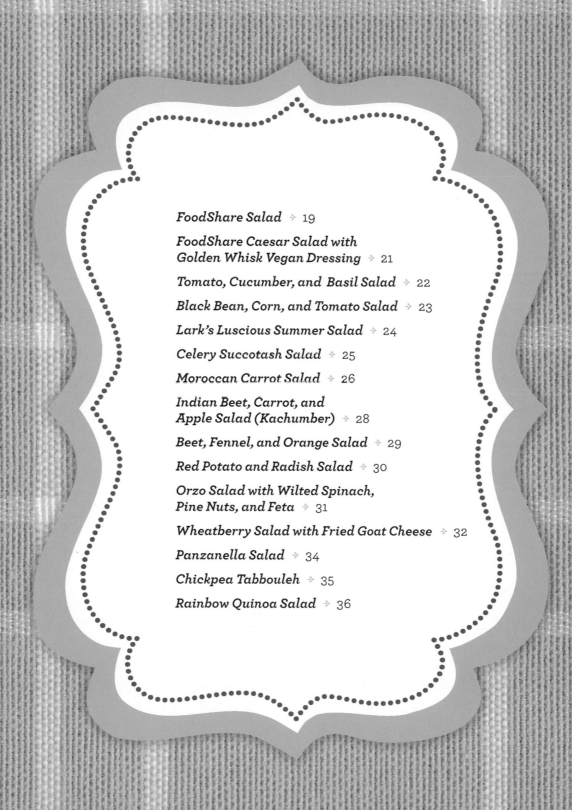

growing

The smell of a just-picked tomato, the sweetness of an Ontario strawberry in June, and the satisfaction of eating food that we have grown ourselves are among the most profound delights of living. Students are inspired by food they planted themselves, high-rise residents are proud they can provide organic food for their children, people with mental health issues have a reason to get out of bed to tend to their gardens: these are all stories FoodShare hears because of our programs to grow food.

FoodShare promotes community gardening and urban agriculture every-where—from the grounds of social housing complexes to abandoned lots and from schoolyards to city parks—where gardeners can grow food for their families, build communities, beautify neighbourhoods, and learn about nature's cycles. Facilitating gardens in Toronto community housing and co-op buildings was one of FoodShare's first programs and we continue to support community gardens through our community food animators, who provide training and work-shops. FoodShare's manual *How Does Our Garden Grow? A Guide to Community Garden Success*, by Laura Berman, is the first of its kind in Canada and has helped to start community gardens all across the country.

Our mid-scale composting operation produces over 25,000 pounds of the city's best compost every year, processing all our kitchen and warehouse scraps—even meat, grease, and bones along with vegetables and fruit—to feed our gardens.

In our onsite greenhouse and demonstration gardens, we grow hundreds of pounds of organic food for our kitchen and teach children and community members how easy it is to grow bounties in small spaces. We also work actively in a number of growing partnerships, among them the Toronto Community Garden Network and Toronto Urban Growers, and support urban beehives in partnership with the Toronto Beekeepers Co-operative. Working with the Centre for Addiction and Mental Health, we run the Sunshine Garden, Toronto's first market garden, and with teachers and students we facilitate the Bendale Market Garden, the city's first school market garden, at Bendale Business and Technical Institute.

When Zahra Parvinian, FoodShare's director of social enterprise, visited southern Iran as a child, her grandmother would always say, "Eat from the rain-bow each day." Nutritional food guides around the world confirm this age-old advice. And so from all our gardens to your kitchen, here is a great set of salads to make it easy to eat green, yellow, red, and all the colours of the rainbow.

FoodShare Salad

Chefs Jesús Gomez, Sybil Pinnock, and Alvin Rebick make the FoodShare kitchen a hub of warmth, excitement, and learning, cooking up creative dishes every day and modelling FoodShare's vision of Good Healthy Food for All by serving fresh, healthy, affordable, multiculturally sensitive food to our family of staff, volunteers, and guests and through their successful catering company, Field to Table Catering. The team received the Bhayana Family Foundation Team Achievement Award in 2009.

Not a day goes by when a FoodShare lunch is not accompanied by a green salad. The elements change with the seasons: tomato, sweet red pepper, and radish in the summer months give way to carrots and purple cabbage in the fall. No matter what the ingredients, the preparation, presentation, and pleasure taken in the eating are always the same. Our house dressing is a FoodShare favourite, with its delicate balance of tart and sweet. This recipe will make more dressing than you need for one salad, and it will keep well in the fridge.

Dressing

3 tbsp rice vinegar

3 tbsp orange juice

2 tsp Dijon mustard

2 tsp maple syrup

½ cup extra virgin olive oil

¼ tsp salt, or to taste

**⅛ tsp freshly ground
black pepper**

Salad

**1 head romaine or leaf lettuce,
torn in bite-sized pieces**

**½ English cucumber, quartered
lengthwise and sliced**

**1 sweet red pepper, seeded
and diced**

1 carrot, shredded

For dressing, in small bowl, whisk together vinegar, orange juice, mustard, and maple syrup. Whisking constantly, slowly drizzle in oil. Whisk in salt and pepper.

To assemble, place lettuce pieces in large bowl. Garnish with cucumber, red pepper, and carrot. Toss with enough dressing to coat lightly.

Makes 4 servings.

FoodShare Caesar Salad
with Golden Whisk Vegan Dressing

Caesar salad is always a treat, and though it may seem fancy, it's quite simple to make. The classic Caesar is romaine lettuce, croutons, and the namesake dressing, often with a sprinkle of Parmesan cheese, but at FoodShare, with the help of holistic nutritionist and chef Katie Compton, we have reinvented it by substituting toasted pepitas for the croutons and making a delicious (and nutritious!) creamy salad dressing with tofu so that everyone can enjoy it. Vegan Worcestershire sauce is available at some health food stores.

Developed to dazzle the taste buds of Grade 7 and 8 students in FoodShare's Good Food Café, this vegan Caesar salad dressing is such a revelation that it won a Toronto Star Golden Whisk Award in 2009. When not dressing romaine lettuce, it can be served as a dip with crudités. This recipe will make more dressing than you need for one salad, and will keep well in the fridge.

Dressing

¾ cup (about 6½ oz/185 g) silken tofu

¼ cup extra virgin olive oil

3 tbsp fresh lemon juice

1 tbsp finely chopped garlic
(about 2 large cloves)

1 tbsp red wine vinegar

1 tbsp white (shiro) miso paste

1 tsp Dijon mustard

1 tsp vegan Worcestershire sauce

½ tsp sea salt

¼ tsp freshly ground black pepper

Salad

⅓ cup pepitas (hulled pumpkin
seeds)

1 large head romaine lettuce, torn
into bite-sized pieces

Fresh lemon juice (optional)

For dressing, place all ingredients in food processor or blender; process until smooth.

For salad, lightly toast pepitas in dry frying pan on medium heat, being careful not to burn, about 4 to 5 minutes. Remove from the heat and let rest on a plate. Place lettuce in a salad bowl and toss with about ½ cup of the salad dressing. Add extra lemon juice, if you like, and sprinkle the top with the toasted pepitas.

Makes 4 servings.

Tomato, Cucumber, and Basil Salad

This simple salad comes from David Kraft, a consultant for non-profits and husband of FoodShare executive director Debbie Field. David says it reminds him of his Kitchener grandparents, whose massive summer garden fed family and friends.

Children love this salad and it can be served many times a week when tomatoes are in season. It is also appetizing made in the middle of February with locally grown greenhouse tomatoes, cucumbers, and basil. Try this versatile salad with the addition of your own favourite ingredients or freshly harvested bounty.

4 tomatoes

4 small pickling cucumbers, peeled

1 cup coarsely chopped fresh basil leaves

5 tbsp olive oil

Juice of ½ lemon (about 2 tbsp)

2 tbsp low-sodium soy sauce

Slice tomatoes and arrange in a single layer around the rim of a large plate. Slice cucumbers and pile in the centre of the tomatoes, being sure to keep a border of tomato exposed. Sprinkle basil on top of cucumbers.

Drizzle oil evenly over the entire salad, followed by lemon juice and soy sauce.

Makes 4 servings.

Black Bean, Corn, and Tomato Salad

Ravenna Nuaimy-Barker learned this recipe in her first year of university and has relied on it ever since for a fast and easy summer meal. Ravenna is now the director of Sustain Ontario, but in her work at FoodShare she played a major role in bringing to life city-wide community food programs and also helped build our landmark mid-scale composting program, which makes it possible for city dwellers in apartments and social housing to turn waste into soil for community gardens.

This is a great dish for summer barbecues or potlucks, when tomatoes are in season. You can use canned or frozen corn, but it is best with fresh corn cut off the cob. Don't make ahead or it will become watery.

Dressing

3 tbsp fresh lime or lemon juice

¼ cup extra virgin olive oil

2 cloves garlic, finely chopped

½ cup chopped fresh coriander

¼ tsp salt

Salad

2 cans (19 oz/540 mL each) black beans, rinsed and drained

3 cups chopped tomatoes

2½ cups fresh or frozen corn kernels

¼ cup finely chopped red onion

For dressing, in small bowl whisk together lime juice, oil, garlic, coriander, and salt.

In large bowl, stir together beans, tomatoes, corn, and red onion. Pour dressing over; toss to coat. Taste; add more salt if necessary.

Serve at room temperature.

Makes about 8 servings.

Lark's Luscious Summer Salad

Lark Kerr, a volunteer co-ordinator of a community Good Food Box drop-off location, sends the recipe for this refreshing salad inspired by the contents of a summer Good Food Box. Lark tells us, "I created this delectable salad, which is now my most favourite ever." One of the many pleasures of getting the Good Food Box is the way the product mix varies depending on the season and the best prices we can get for a range of produce. Serve this salad as is or on a bed of your favourite leafy salad greens.

½ **canary yellow melon, cantaloupe, or honeydew melon, seeded, peeled, cut in bite-sized chunks**

1 **ripe avocado, pitted, peeled, cut in bite-sized chunks**

1 **ripe mango, pitted, peeled, cut in bite-sized chunks**

¼ **small red onion, finely chopped (about 1 tbsp)**

Juice of 1 lime (about 2 tbsp)

1 **tbsp grated ginger root**

1 **tbsp chopped fresh mint**

In medium bowl, combine all ingredients; toss to combine.

Makes about 4 servings.

Celery Succotash Salad

In 2009, a Grade 7 and 8 middle school moved into the former high school in which FoodShare has its offices, greenhouse, gardens, and fresh produce warehouse. A few of the parents suggested that we begin cooking lunch for the 140 students, and our healthy school cafeteria, the Good Food Café, was born.

This salad is a favourite in the Good Food Café. It is crunchy and colourful and uses numerous vegetables. It's also a great recipe for training the Focus on Food youth interns who learn job skills while working in our kitchen because, since we prepare it in large quantities, there's lots of chopping to do. The Good Food Café has taught us that students will try healthy food if it looks and smells good. It has also taught FoodShare that students are more inclined to try a healthy salad like this one if it is prepared and served to them by a young person.

Dressing

1 tbsp Dijon mustard
1 tbsp honey
Juice of 1 lemon (about 3–4 tbsp)
1 tbsp red wine vinegar
¼ cup olive oil

Salad

4 stalks celery, thinly sliced
1 carrot, shredded (about ½ cup)
2 cups fresh or frozen corn kernels
1 sweet red pepper, diced
2 green onions, finely chopped
1 can (19 oz/540 mL) chickpeas, rinsed and drained
Salt and freshly ground black pepper to taste

For dressing, in small bowl whisk together mustard, honey, lemon juice, vinegar, and oil.

For salad, in large bowl combine celery, carrot, corn, pepper, green onions, and chickpeas.

Toss dressing with vegetables and season with salt and pepper.

Serve immediately or refrigerate up to 2 days.

Makes about 6 servings.

Moroccan Carrot Salad

The great thing about carrots is how long they last. Long after other fresh produce in your fridge is gone, carrots will still taste fresh and crisp. At FoodShare we are lucky to have access to carrots almost year round, since Ontario is one of the few places in the world where carrots are stored for up to twelve months. We buy certified organic carrots from Pfenning's Organic Farm in Baden, Ontario, and multicoloured heritage carrots from Jason Verkaik of Carron Farms, a Local Food Plus (LFP) certified farm in the Holland Marsh, for our Good Food Boxes and to be sold in our Fresh Produce for Schools and Community Agencies program. In both cases, these farmers drive their produce directly to the door of FoodShare's Field to Table Community Food Hub. Colourful carrots are a real hit in student nutrition programs. This flavour-packed salad is a favourite creation of the FoodShare kitchen.

¼ **cup unsweetened finely shredded coconut**

¼ **cup olive oil**

1 tsp ground cumin

3 large carrots, shredded

Juice of 1 lemon (about 3–4 tbsp)

½ **cup raisins**

Pinch cinnamon

Pinch granulated sugar

In dry frying pan, gently toast coconut on medium heat until it just starts to change to a light brown, about 3 to 4 minutes. Transfer to a plate and set aside.

In same frying pan, heat 1 tablespoon of the oil on medium heat and add cumin. Toast cumin in the oil, watching closely and stirring gently to be sure not to let it burn, about 2 minutes. Remove from heat.

Place carrots in a medium bowl. Add the remaining oil and toasted cumin and stir to combine. Cool briefly. Add lemon juice, raisins, cinnamon, sugar, and coconut and mix well.

Makes 4 servings.

Indian Beet, Carrot, and Apple Salad (Kachumber)

From Preena Chauhan, a Toronto Food Policy Council member who combines a commitment to food culture with business. Through Arvinda's Indian Cooking Classes, she and her mother provide a gateway to classical Indian cooking and also sell unique artisanal spice blends based on traditional Indian recipes but packaged in Canada.

Preena says, "I love this recipe for its beauty and its simplicity. A kachumber is a salad of raw vegetables, but in Indian cuisine, we don't have a salad course." Instead, serve this beautiful dish on the side with a spicy meal to refresh the palate. As the salad sits, the beet colour bleeds into the entire dish, so serve immediately to enjoy the contrasting hues of apple and carrot. Use large holes on a box grater to shred the vegetables and fruit. Garam masala is a mild spice mixture sold in Indian food shops.

Salad
3 medium or 2 large beets, shredded
2 large carrots, shredded
2 apples, peeled and shredded

Dressing
2 tbsp red wine vinegar
1 tbsp fresh lime or lemon juice
2 tsp granulated sugar
½ tsp sea or kosher salt
¼ tsp garam masala

Garnish
¼ cup finely chopped fresh coriander
¼ large red onion, sliced in thin rings

In large bowl, toss together beets, carrots, and apples.

For dressing, in small bowl combine vinegar, lime juice, sugar, salt, and garam masala. Pour over beet mixture; toss to coat.

Serve garnished with coriander and onion rings.

Makes 6 to 8 servings.

Beet, Fennel, and Orange Salad

This is gorgeous as a lunch, side salad, or dinner party appetizer. FoodShare's Field to Table Catering, one of Canada's first food-related social enterprises, caters for occasions small and large, from community events to weddings and conferences, providing the same dishes served at FoodShare daily. We are often asked for this favourite.

Salad

3 beets

1 tbsp olive oil

Pinch each: salt and freshly ground black pepper

2 oranges

1 bulb fennel, thinly sliced

3 cups baby arugula

Dressing

1 tbsp red wine vinegar

1 tsp Dijon mustard

1 clove garlic, finely chopped

¼ tsp each: salt and freshly ground black pepper

⅓ cup extra virgin olive oil

Salt and freshly ground pepper to taste

Place beets in large saucepan with cold salted water to cover. Cover and bring to a boil. Reduce heat to medium-high and cook, partially covered, for 40 to 50 minutes or until beets are tender when pierced with tip of sharp knife.

Meanwhile, preheat oven to 400°F (200°C).

Drain cooked beets. Peel under cold running water. Cut each beet into 8 wedges. Toss with oil, salt, and pepper. Place in single layer on rimmed baking sheet. Roast in centre of oven for 20 minutes. Set aside to cool.

One at a time, hold oranges over a large bowl to catch juice and, using small paring knife, cut away rind and pith; cut between membrane and pulp to release segments. Set orange segments aside. Measure out and reserve 1 tablespoon of the orange juice.

For dressing, in small bowl, whisk together reserved orange juice, vinegar, mustard, garlic, salt, and pepper. Whisk in oil until smooth.

In large bowl containing orange segments and any remaining juice, add cooled beets, sliced fennel, and dressing, and gently toss. Season with salt and pepper.

Divide arugula among 6 plates; spoon beet salad on top.

Makes 6 servings.

Red Potato and Radish Salad

In the Montreal district of Hochelaga-Maisonneuve, three women began cooking together in 1985 to save money, buying food in bulk and enjoying the pleasure of making food as a group. Diane Norman, a nutritionist in their neighbourhood, helped take the idea further with a model based on the comedores populares of Peru. Community kitchens came to Toronto in 1991 when Diane visited FoodShare, and that first meeting formed the basis of the community cooking programs we offer to this day, building community and individual capacity through hands-on food skills.

This is a popular recipe in Fairview Community Health Centre's community kitchen during the hot summer months. It's a great alternative to a more conventional potato salad since it doesn't include mayonnaise, which makes it healthier and ideal for picnics, when mayonnaise can spoil quickly.

24 baby red-skinned potatoes (about 3 lb/1.5 kg), cut in half

½ cup vegetable oil

¼ cup fresh lemon juice

1 tbsp Dijon or grainy mustard

½ tsp salt

½ tsp freshly ground black pepper

¼ tsp granulated sugar

12 radishes, thinly sliced

2 stalks celery, diced

½ red onion, thinly sliced (about ½ cup)

¼ cup chopped fresh dill

Place potatoes in medium saucepan with cold water to cover. Cover and bring to a boil. Reduce heat and simmer 7 to 10 minutes or until potatoes are tender. Drain and cool.

In large bowl, whisk together oil, lemon juice, mustard, salt, pepper, and sugar. Add potatoes, radishes, celery, onion, and dill; toss gently to combine.

Serve immediately or refrigerate up to 2 days.

Makes about 8 servings.

Orzo Salad with Wilted Spinach, Pine Nuts, and Feta

A terrific pasta salad idea for a potluck meal. Dusanka Pavlica of Canadian Feed the Children contributed this favourite, telling us, "Many, many years ago, as a new mom, I was blessed to meet a great community of mothers on a web board. One of the ties that bound us was our love of food and Sandra from Colorado gave me this recipe. I often add extra spinach, and my daughter Maja likes it with a healthy squeeze of lemon or lime and some freshly ground pepper."

1 package (1 lb/500 g) orzo

½ cup olive oil

2 tbsp butter

½ tsp finely chopped garlic

½ tsp dried basil

½ tsp hot pepper flakes

1 cup pine nuts

1 package (10 oz/300 g) baby spinach

Salt to taste

2 tbsp balsamic vinegar

8 oz (250 g) feta cheese, crumbled (about 2 cups)

1 tomato, chopped

In large saucepan of boiling salted water, cook orzo for 8 to 10 minutes or until tender. Drain and transfer to large bowl.

In large frying pan, heat oil and butter over medium-high heat until butter melts. Add garlic, basil, and pepper flakes; cook, stirring, for 30 seconds or until blended and fragrant. Reduce heat to medium and stir in pine nuts. Cook, stirring frequently, until lightly browned, about 4 minutes. Stir in spinach. Reduce heat to low, cover, and cook for 5 minutes or until spinach is wilted. Add to orzo; toss to mix and add salt.

Divide among dinner plates. Drizzle with vinegar. Sprinkle with feta and tomato.

Makes 8 to 10 servings.

Wheatberry Salad with Fried Goat Cheese

An elegant appetizer salad from Marc Breton, local food hero, champion of Food Literacy for students, and former executive chef of the Gladstone Hotel. Mark says it was important to him to contribute to this cookbook: "I have three children (grown up now) and the pleasure of simple, healthy food has to start with kids."

This salad is a favourite because "it tastes great, fresh; and with the grains, lentils, and cheese it makes a good vegetarian meal with complete proteins." Serve on a bed of lettuce, if desired. Use Woolwich, Montforte, or other soft goat cheese log. The goat cheese rounds could be a nice addition to almost any salad.

Salad

1 lb (500 g) beets
⅓ cup dried green lentils
⅓ cup wheatberries
1 English cucumber, diced
1 shallot, finely chopped
1 tbsp chopped fresh parsley

Dressing

2 tbsp fresh lemon juice
2 tbsp white wine vinegar
1 tbsp Dijon mustard
1 tsp maple syrup
¼ cup extra virgin olive oil
Salt and freshly ground black pepper to taste

Goat Cheese Rounds

7 oz (about 200 g) soft unripened goat cheese log
Vegetable oil
¼ cup all-purpose flour
1 egg, beaten
½ cup dry breadcrumbs or panko

Preheat oven to 425°F (220°C).

If beets have greens, remove them, leaving about ¼ inch (5 mm) of stems. Scrub the beets and place in a baking dish or oven-proof casserole dish with lid. Add ¼ inch (5 mm) of water to the dish. Cover tightly. Place in the oven and roast until tender when pierced with tip of knife, 30 to 40 minutes for small beets, 40 to 45 minutes for medium beets, and 50 to 60 minutes for large beets. Set aside in covered dish until cool enough to handle.

Meanwhile, cover lentils and wheatberries with 2 inches (5 cm) cold water in separate small saucepans. Bring to a boil. Reduce heat and simmer until tender, about 20 minutes for lentils and 30 minutes for wheatberries. Drain and spread out on rimmed baking sheet to cool.

While beets are still warm, cut away the ends and slip off the skins. Cut in small dice about the same size as the cucumber. In large bowl, toss together beets, lentils, wheatberries, cucumber, shallot, and parsley.

For dressing, in small jar place lemon juice, vinegar, mustard, maple syrup, and oil. Cover jar tightly; shake until combined. Add salt and pepper. Pour over wheatberry mixture; toss to coat.

For goat cheese rounds, cut log crosswise into equal portions to form 6 discs. Pour oil into frying pan to depth of ¾ inch (2 cm). Heat over medium heat. Dredge goat cheese discs in flour, dip in beaten egg, and dredge in breadcrumbs. Carefully place in hot oil. Fry until golden, about 2 minutes, turning halfway. Drain on paper towel.

Divide salad among 6 plates; top each with a warm goat cheese round.

Makes 6 servings.

Today I learned that soil is too important to treat like dirt.
GRADE 2 STUDENT AFTER A
FOOD LITERACY WORKSHOP

share * salads

33

Panzanella Salad

Marion Kane was inspired by American TV chef Tyler Florence to adapt this version of an Italian bread salad that uses crisp croutons instead of plain bread. Aromatic and beautiful as a summer side dish or a light main course.

Dressing

2 cloves garlic

3 anchovy fillets

¼ tsp each: kosher salt and freshly ground black pepper

Juice of ½ lemon (about 2 tbsp)

2 tbsp red wine vinegar

⅓ cup extra virgin olive oil

1 tbsp drained capers (optional)

Salad

2 sweet red peppers

8 cups Italian bread cut in 1-inch (2.5 cm) cubes (about ½ loaf)

¼ cup extra virgin olive oil

2 cups cherry or grape tomatoes, cut in half

½ small red onion, chopped

1 English cucumber, peeled, cut in ½-inch (1 cm) cubes

½ cup fresh basil leaves, torn in pieces

¼ cup chopped fresh parsley

Preheat broiler.

For dressing, finely chop garlic, anchovies, salt, and pepper together on cutting board, then mash with side of large chef knife. Transfer to small bowl; whisk in lemon juice, vinegar, and oil. Stir in capers (if using).

Place peppers on rimmed baking sheet under broiler. Broil about 15 minutes, turning at intervals, until charred and blistered all over. (Alternatively, place on barbecue grill preheated to medium-high.) Place in bowl, cover with plastic wrap, and let stand about 10 minutes. Peel off skin; remove stems and seeds and discard. Chop peppers into bite-sized pieces.

Preheat oven to 400°F (200°C).

Place bread cubes in large bowl. Toss with oil. Spread in single layer on rimmed baking sheet. Bake in centre of oven for 10 minutes or until crisp and golden.

In large bowl, combine roasted peppers, tomatoes, red onion, cucumber, and basil. Add dressing; toss to coat. Just before serving, add toasted bread; toss together. Add additional salt and pepper if necessary. Serve sprinkled with parsley.

Makes about 6 servings.

Chickpea Tabbouleh

This variation on the traditional version of tabbouleh comes from Voula Halliday, who served it in the Dundas Street Public School lunch program. Canada is the only G8 country and one of the few countries in the world without a federal school food policy, so parents and teachers organize school food programs one school at a time. Since 1991, Dundas Street has been a model of a food-mobilized school, with breakfast, lunch, snack, and after-school programs all serving wholesome food and everyone—students, parents, caretakers, teachers, and the principal—pitching in to make the programs a success.

Voula—a parent and chef and now one of the co-chairs of Toronto's Slow Food convivium—was the cook at Dundas Street Public School for two years, ordering local produce through FoodShare's Fresh Produce for Schools and Community Agencies program, proving daily that children will eat healthy food if it is prepared in an appealing way.

1 cup fine quick-cooking bulgur

1 large tomato, diced

3 green onions, finely chopped

1 cup coarsely chopped flat-leaf parsley

½ English cucumber, seeded and diced

1 cup cooked chickpeas or about ½ can (19 oz/540mL), rinsed and drained

⅓ cup fresh lemon juice (juice of 2–3 lemons)

3 tbsp olive oil

¼ tsp each: salt and freshly ground black pepper

In small saucepan, combine bulgur with 2 cups water. Bring to a boil, cover, turn off heat, and let sit until soft, about 4 minutes. Fluff with a fork, transfer to medium bowl; add tomato, green onions, parsley, cucumber, and chickpeas.

In small bowl, whisk together lemon juice, oil, salt, and pepper. Pour over bulgur mixture; toss to combine. Refrigerate for 1 hour and toss again before serving.

Makes about 6 servings.

Rainbow Quinoa Salad

From Tammara Soma of the Toronto Youth Food Policy Council and Sustain Ontario, who says, "When I first tried quinoa it was love at first sight. It is one of the most versatile ingredients ever and best of all, my three-year-old son asks for it!" Quinoa is a nutritious grain that is high in protein. It can be found in health food stores and many supermarkets. The white variety is more commonly available but there is also a red variety; use either. Omit rinsing step if the package directions say it is not necessary.

Salad

1 cup quinoa, rinsed and drained

Pinch salt

1 cup chopped seedless cucumber

1 cup dried cranberries

1 can (14 oz/398 mL) chickpeas, rinsed and drained

2 carrots, shredded

¼ cup chopped fresh mint

¼ cup chopped fresh parsley

Dressing

⅔ cup extra virgin olive oil

2 tbsp fresh lemon juice

2 tbsp fresh lime juice

½ tsp salt

Freshly ground black pepper to taste

In saucepan, bring 2 cups water to a boil. Stir in quinoa and salt. Reduce heat to medium-low, cover, and cook for 15 minutes or until liquid is absorbed. Remove from heat and let stand for 5 minutes. Fluff with fork. Transfer to large bowl; cool to room temperature.

Stir in cucumber, cranberries, chickpeas, carrots, mint, and parsley.

For dressing, in small bowl, whisk together oil, lemon juice, lime juice, and salt. Pour over salad; toss to coat. Add pepper.

Makes about 6 servings.

Signature Salads:
A Field to Table Schools Activity

This activity is possibly the most popular workshop in FoodShare's Field to Table Schools program. Created by program co-ordinator Brooke Ziebell, it gets students of all ages excited about fresh, healthy food every time. When she leads the activity, Brooke brings a whole class of students together and allows them to make their own signature salad.

PREPARATION

Have ready some small mason jars or other jars suitable for shaking (with tight lids). Gather a selection of ingredients from some or all of the groups listed below. The ingredients given are just a starting point.

SALAD

- Fresh vegetables: chard, lettuces, kale, beets, carrots, onions, beans, peas, herbs, peppers, avocados, tomatoes
- Fruits: apples, pears, grapes, cantaloupes, mangoes
- Whole grains: bread, pasta, rice, bulgur, barley, quinoa
- Proteins (optional): seeds, nuts, legumes, cheeses, cottage cheese

DRESSING

- Oil component: olive oil, canola oil, sunflower oil, sesame oil
- Acidic component: apple cider vinegar, balsamic vinegar, lemons, limes, oranges
- Sweet component: honey, maple syrup, apple juice
- Salty component: salt, soy sauce, olive brine
- Creamy component (optional): silken tofu, plain yogurt
- Spicy component (optional): cumin, paprika, chili sauce
- Herb component (optional): basil, oregano, dill, fresh coriander, sage, rosemary

DIRECTIONS

In this activity, you are going to choose from the selection of all of the ingredients on hand to create your very own signature salad! Try to use different preparation techniques, such as grating, slicing, dicing, or tearing.

Your challenge, if you choose to accept it, is to create an original salad with at least three different

- colours
- textures
- food groups
- locally grown ingredients.

For the dressing, begin by filling your jar one-third full with the oil of your choice. The oil is usually the most abundant salad dressing ingredient unless you're using sesame oil, in which case a few drops or a splash in addition to another, less flavourful oil is ideal.

Now you get to select the acidic ingredient of your choice. This provides lots of opportunity to build new kitchen skills, such as

- squeezing lemons over clean hands to stop any seeds from going into the bowl while releasing the juice
- using a measuring cup to measure ingredients
- estimating to what level on a jar to pour vinegar.

Now it's time for something sweet. Be careful here, as you may be tempted to add more sweet ingredients than you need. Your dressing should balance all the flavours, and no one taste should dominate. Again, there's opportunity for learning at this step, such as

- using measuring spoons
- heating crystallized honey gently on the stovetop to liquefy before adding to the jar.

Finally, it's time to add something salty to enhance the overall flavour. Too much salt can be damaging to your health, so it's important to use moderation at this step. Some fun kitchen skills to learn here are

- adding "a pinch" of an ingredient
- adding salt "to taste," first a little bit and then tasting and adjusting as necessary.

Remember, you can always add more if needed, but once you add too much, it's difficult to reverse.

Adding something creamy or spicy is optional.

The next and most important step is to taste the dressing. Remember, the flavour will be much more powerful by itself than when the mixture is used as a dressing with salad. Check for the balance of flavours.

Finally, add the dressing to your fresh salad and enjoy with your friends!

soups

 Cooking is fundamental to who we are as people, families, and cultures. Sharing recipes through the generations, teaching our children how to cook from scratch so that they are self-sufficient in a world of prepared foods, and making delicious food without spending a fortune are important personal and political acts. Taking control over what we put in our own bodies and those of our families for joy and health depends on being able to cook.

Cooking, and our kitchen, is at the heart of FoodShare. Every day our kitchen staff lovingly prepare and serve fresh, affordable, multiculturally sensitive food. A hub of learning, FoodShare's kitchen has many functions: it provides hands-on capacity building through hundreds of cooking and budgeting workshops; it prepares nutrient-dense Power Soups that are delivered by community agencies to the homeless; it supports more than 50 community kitchens across the city; it houses our Baby and Toddler Nutrition program, whose peer trainers support parents in 8 languages; it models the preparation of healthy, sustainable food through our award-winning Field to Table Catering; it prepares meals each day for staff, volunteers, guests, and Grade 7 and 8 students through the Good Food Café; and, working closely with the Good Food programs, it provides employment experience and life skills training for youth in our Focus on Food internship program.

For many, cooking from scratch seems very hard, and making soup can seem impossible, almost magical. For Alvin Rebick, FoodShare's kitchen manager, making soup is fun: "In many ways soup is the perfect food—simple, nutritious, and delicious." He recommends experimenting with what's left in your fridge and adding a little of this and a little of that.

So from our kitchen to yours, some great soups to comfort you on a cold day, cool you on a hot day, heal you when you are not feeling well, and to feed family and friends.

Yogurt Cucumber Soup with Walnuts (Tarator)

From Mariya Misheva, a Good Food Box co-ordinator, comes this refreshing Ukrainian classic, which she says was her father's favourite. Good Food Boxes are distributed through neighbourhood drop-off sites across the city—front porches, apartments, community agencies, churches, and more—each drop organized by a volunteer. It is quite a complicated job as the co-ordinator collects money before placing the order with FoodShare and has to make sure that all the people at their drop-off, usually 10 to 15 neighbours, remember to pick up their boxes after the driver makes the delivery. As a small thanks for the effort, each co-ordinator receives one free Good Food Box per delivery.

This cold soup is perfect for a summer day but also a lovely pick-me-up all year round. Natural yogurt is made without thickeners.

4 cups plain natural yogurt

2 cloves garlic

1 tsp salt

½ cup walnut halves

¼ cup olive oil

1 English cucumber, peeled, seeded, finely chopped

1 tbsp balsamic vinegar (optional)

Sprig of mint (optional)

In large bowl, stir together yogurt and ½ cup cold water.

Finely chop garlic together with salt on cutting board, then mash into a paste with side of large chef knife. Stir into yogurt.

In mortar, pound walnuts to a paste using a pestle. Gradually add oil, continuing to mash until it is all worked into walnut paste. Stir into yogurt mixture. Stir cucumber into yogurt. Cover and refrigerate several hours or overnight.

Before serving, stir in balsamic vinegar (if using) and thin with ½ cup cold water if soup is too thick. Serve in chilled bowls. Garnish with sprig of mint (if using).

Makes about 6 servings.

Gazpacho

This Spanish-inspired cold soup comes from Toronto food writer, stylist, and devotee of good food Heather Trim. It's a cinch to make and wonderfully refreshing. This calls for 6 cups of vegetable cocktail, which is a 1.5 litre jar.

2 large tomatoes, cut in chunks

1 sweet yellow, red, or green pepper, cut in chunks

1 large English cucumber or 2 field cucumbers, seeded and cut in chunks

2 cloves garlic, finely chopped

6 cups vegetable cocktail or tomato juice

4 green onions, chopped

¼ cup red wine vinegar

½ tsp hot pepper sauce, or to taste

Salt and freshly ground black pepper to taste

Croutons, homemade or store bought (optional)

In food processor or blender, combine tomatoes, pepper, cucumber, and garlic. Pulse on and off until evenly and coarsely chopped but not puréed. Transfer to large bowl. Stir in vegetable cocktail, green onions, vinegar, hot pepper sauce, salt, and pepper. Refrigerate at least 1 hour.

Serve cold, garnished with croutons (if using).

Makes about 8 servings.

One of my favourite things is that the staff eats together. The act of eating together values food as something that can bring community together. . . . Also the universal aspect of FoodShare programs diminishes or even eliminates stigma for those people who really need the programs.
YORK UNIVERSITY STUDENT AFTER A VISIT TO FOODSHARE'S FIELD TO TABLE COMMUNITY FOOD HUB

Curried Roasted Squash Soup

There is nothing like the texture of a puréed vegetable soup. Smooth and sensuous, a soup such as this one is a pleasure to eat. Roasting the vegetables with the spices intensifies the flavours, and the addition of coconut milk adds a unique sweetness. Easy, elegant, and beautiful to look at, this soup provided by FoodShare chef Alvin Rebick is a fall and winter winner, a warm and nourishing staff favourite. It is also an important staple in the Power Soups program, which serves nutrient-dense puréed meals to the homeless and under-housed in the cold winter months.

1 butternut squash, peeled,
    seeded, cut in large chunks

3 onions, cut in wedges

2 carrots, chopped

3 cloves garlic

2 tbsp curry powder

2 tbsp ground cumin

1 tsp cinnamon

Pinch cayenne pepper

¼ cup vegetable oil

8 cups vegetable stock or water

1 can (14 oz/398 mL) coconut milk

½ cup chopped fresh coriander

Salt to taste

Preheat oven to 350°F (180°C). Line large rimmed baking sheet with parchment paper.

In large bowl, toss squash, onions, carrots, garlic, curry powder, cumin, cinnamon, and cayenne with oil. Spread on baking sheet and bake for 30 minutes.

Transfer vegetables to large soup pot and add stock and coconut milk. Bring to a boil. Add coriander; reduce heat and simmer uncovered for 30 minutes.

Season with salt and remove from heat. Using food processor, blender, or immersion blender, purée until smooth.

Serve immediately or return to pot and keep warm on low heat.

Makes 6 servings.

Red Lentil and Spinach Soup

FoodShare has a wonderful Baby and Toddler Nutrition program to teach parents how to feed their children healthy, fresh, affordable food with ease and confidence. No matter what the culture (our peer trainers teach workshops in 8 different languages), each new generation faces the daunting challenge of feeding their children. FoodShare's kitchen manager Alvin Rebick got involved in this program at the same time that his daughter Terra became a mother. Despite having two parents who are chefs, she needed reassurance about the best foods for young Rosie, and Alvin took the principles of FoodShare's program and passed them along to her.

Becoming a grandfather (Gaga) was an inspiration for Alvin as well. Every Saturday on his return from the market, he makes a soup for his family to eat the following week. His grandchildren are his biggest soup fans and the recipe that follows is one of their favourites, which they call "Gaga's Lentil Soup."

1 tbsp vegetable oil

1 onion, diced

2 stalks celery, diced

2 carrots, diced

2 cups dried red lentils, rinsed and drained

1 tsp ground cumin

2 tsp curry powder

1 tsp each: salt and freshly ground black pepper

12 cups vegetable stock or water or combination

6 cups fresh chopped spinach or 1 cup cooked frozen

1 cup chopped fresh coriander

In large saucepan, heat oil on medium and sauté onion, celery, and carrots for 5 minutes. Add lentils, cumin, curry powder, salt, and pepper. Stir to coat vegetables and lentils with spices.

Add stock, spinach, and coriander. Bring to a boil. Reduce heat and simmer for 20 minutes or until lentils are soft.

Makes 8 servings.

Mushroom Barley Soup

This hearty vegetarian soup is surprisingly rich and meaty tasting, another winner from FoodShare's kitchen and a favourite in our Good Food Box newsletters. The newsletters always include at least one recipe using the week's featured vegetable or fruit, an item some may not have encountered before.

¼ cup butter

5 cups chopped mushrooms (about 1 lb/500 g)

2 carrots, chopped

2 stalks celery, chopped

1 onion, chopped

½ cup pearl barley, rinsed and drained

2 tbsp all-purpose flour

6 cups water or vegetable stock

Salt and freshly ground black pepper to taste

¼ cup chopped fresh dill or parsley (optional)

In large saucepan, melt butter over medium-high heat. Add mushrooms, carrots, celery, onion, and barley; cook until vegetables start to brown, stirring often, about 10 minutes. Add flour; cook for 5 minutes, stirring. Gradually stir in water or stock. Bring to a boil. Reduce heat to low and simmer uncovered until barley is tender, about 40 minutes.

Add salt and pepper. Stir in chopped herbs (if using).

Makes about 6 servings.

Borscht

This borscht recipe is from Lori Stahlbrand's grandmother, her Babu, who came to Canada in 1912 from Bukovina, Ukraine. Lori is the founder of Local Food Plus (LFP), which certifies farmers who reduce pesticides, treat their animals well, conserve soil and water, protect wildlife habitat, provide safe and fair working conditions, reduce energy use, and sell locally wherever possible. With Rod MacRae, the first co-ordinator of the Toronto Food Policy Council, and Wayne Roberts, the second TFPC co-ordinator, Lori is the author of Real Food for a Change: Bringing Nature, Health, Joy and Justice to the Table, an important book about the food system in Canada.

"Babu's Borscht" is hearty and inexpensive and can be made with local, sustainable ingredients like those grown by LFP farmers. Although Lori's Babu always served this borscht with cornmeal mush and sour cream and usually made it with meat, the soup can also be made with dried mushrooms for a vegetarian or vegan option. The vegetarian version is traditionally eaten on Ukrainian Christmas (January 6) as one of 12 meatless dishes. If you have a food processor, you can use the shredder blade for the beets, potato, carrot, and cabbage.

1½ lb (750 g) stewing beef, spareribs, brisket, chuck, or shank (omit for vegetarian version)

1 tsp salt

1 onion, chopped

2 cloves garlic, finely chopped

1 bay leaf

3 beets, shredded

1 potato, peeled and shredded

1 carrot, shredded

½ cup chopped celery

3 cups shredded cabbage

1 cup cooked white kidney or navy beans or about ½ can (19 oz/540 mL), rinsed and drained

1 can (28 oz/796 mL) diced tomatoes

Juice of 1 lemon (about 3–4 tbsp)

1 tbsp chopped fresh parsley

1 tbsp chopped fresh dill

Salt and freshly ground black pepper to taste

Cornmeal Mush

1 cup fine cornmeal

½ tsp salt

Sour cream or plain yogurt (optional)

continued on next page

In large saucepan, cover meat with 12 cups of cold water and add salt. Bring to a boil, cover, and reduce heat; simmer for 1½ hours. Skim the foam off the top with a spoon. Remove meat with a slotted spoon and set aside.

To the same saucepan, add onion, garlic, bay leaf, and beets; cook for 10 to 15 minutes. Add potato, carrot, celery, and cabbage; cook until tender but not overcooked.

Return meat to pot. Stir in beans, tomatoes, lemon juice, parsley, and dill. Discard bay leaf. Season with salt and pepper. Warm until beans are heated through.

For cornmeal mush, in medium saucepan bring 2 cups water and ½ teaspoon salt to a rapid boil. Add cornmeal and stir in one direction with a wooden spoon until cornmeal pulls away from the sides of the pan and forms a ball. Transfer onto a dish. It will firm up slightly as it cools.

Serve the borscht and pass around the cornmeal mush so that everyone can put a large scoop of it into the borscht with a dollop of sour cream or plain yogurt (if using) on top.

Makes 6 to 8 servings.

A program for every link in the food chain.

SARAH ELTON, WRITING IN *Locavore: From Farmers' Fields to Rooftop Gardens—How Canadians Are Changing the Way We Eat* ON THE SCOPE FOODSHARE'S WORK

Hearty Minestrone

Chandra Dean and Katie Compton lead Kate's Kitchen, a community kitchen at FoodShare in which survivors of breast cancer come together monthly to cook, talk, and heal. They submitted this recipe because "it best reflects the type of nutritious (and delicious!) food we all cook together every month at FoodShare." You can use canned whole tomatoes and chop them coarsely. The crinkly-leaved Savoy cabbage has a better taste and texture than the more common green cabbage. This soup makes a tasty meal eaten with wholegrain bread.

2 tbsp olive oil

4 cloves garlic, finely chopped

1 onion, chopped

9 cups low-sodium vegetable or chicken stock

1 can (28 oz/796 mL) diced tomatoes

2 large stalks celery, sliced

2 carrots, chopped

1 cup shredded Savoy cabbage

¼ cup tomato paste

¼ cup chopped fresh parsley

1 tbsp chopped fresh basil

1 bay leaf

1 can (19 oz/540 mL) chickpeas, rinsed and drained

1 can (19 oz/540 mL) cannellini or other white beans, rinsed and drained

1 package (5 oz/142 g) baby spinach

Salt and freshly ground black pepper to taste

¾–1 cup grated Parmesan cheese

In large stock pot, heat oil over medium-high heat. Cook garlic and onion for 3 minutes or until translucent. Stir in stock, tomatoes and their juice, celery, carrots, cabbage, tomato paste, parsley, basil, and bay leaf. Bring to a boil. Reduce heat to simmer and cook uncovered for 20 minutes or until vegetables are tender. Stir in chickpeas and beans; simmer another 10 minutes.

Remove from heat. Discard bay leaf. Stir in spinach until it wilts. Add salt and pepper.

Serve sprinkled with Parmesan.

Makes about 8 servings.

Immune-Boosting Soup

This soup from holistic nutritionist, cookbook author, and food TV show host Julie Daniluk, who helped FoodShare start up its Field to Table festival, is fantastic whenever a cold or flu comes knocking. Shiitake mushrooms contain lentinan, an active compound that can boost your immune system. Fresh oregano, rosemary, and thyme contain essential oils that have been shown to be anti-viral and anti-bacterial. Green vegetables like kale, snow peas, and beans contain B vitamins to combat stress. Orange carrots and sweet potatoes are rich in vitamin A, which helps the lungs to fight off infection. Ginger and garlic are powerfully anti-inflammatory.

Leave out the chicken for a vegetarian version of this soup that kept a cold most deliciously at bay for Adrienne while she was working on this book.

2 tbsp olive oil

2 cups finely chopped onion

2 cups chopped leeks (white and tender green part only)

3 tbsp finely chopped ginger root

5 cloves garlic, sliced

2 cups sliced carrots

2 cups chopped shiitake mushroom caps (about 6 oz/175 g whole mushrooms)

2 cups peeled diced sweet potatoes

1 cup sliced celery

4 skinless boneless chicken thighs (about 1 lb/500g), cut in cubes (omit for vegetarian version)

2 bay leaves

8 cups chicken or vegetable stock

4 cups torn kale

1 cup chopped snow peas or green beans

½ cup chopped fresh basil

½ cup chopped fresh parsley

1 tbsp each: chopped fresh oregano, rosemary, and thyme

Salt and freshly ground black pepper to taste

In large stock pot, heat oil over medium heat. Add onion, leeks, ginger, and half the garlic; cook for 3 minutes or until softened. Stir in carrots, mushrooms, sweet potatoes, celery, chicken, bay leaves, and stock. Bring to a boil. Reduce heat to low and cook uncovered for 15 to 20 minutes or until chicken is cooked through and vegetables are tender but not mushy.

Stir in kale, snow peas, basil, parsley, oregano, rosemary, thyme, and remaining garlic. Simmer another 2 minutes or until kale is softened. Discard bay leaves. Add salt and pepper.

Makes about 6 servings.

Chicken Noodle Soup with Matzo Balls

From FoodShare executive director Debbie Field, who got the recipe from her mother, comes this meal-in-a-bowl approach to chicken soup. This makes enough for a large crowd but the recipe can easily be halved. You can either take the skin off the chicken pieces before cooking or leave it on. Some people add parsnip for extra sweetness. If you don't have time to make the matzo balls you can serve the soup with egg noodles.

10 bone-in chicken thighs

10 bone-in chicken drumsticks

6 large carrots, quartered
    lengthwise

6 stalks celery, cut in 1-inch
    (2.5 cm) lengths

2 large onions, quartered

1 bunch fresh dill, chopped

1 bunch fresh parsley, chopped

1 tbsp salt

1½ tsp freshly ground black
    pepper

1 package (10 oz/300 g) fine
    egg noodles (optional)

Matzo Balls

4 eggs

1 cup matzo meal

1 tsp salt

In large stock pot, combine chicken pieces, carrots, celery, onions, dill, parsley, salt, pepper, and 20 cups water. Bring to a boil, skimming off any foam that rises to the surface. Reduce heat to medium-low and cook uncovered for 1½ to 2 hours.

Meanwhile, make matzo balls. Separate eggs. In bowl and using electric mixer, beat egg whites until stiff peaks form. In separate bowl, with fork, lightly beat egg yolks. Fold yolks, matzo meal, and salt into egg whites. Cover bowl; place in freezer for 1 hour.

In saucepan, bring 10 cups of water to a boil; salt lightly. Remove matzo ball batter from freezer. Using wet hands, form into 24 balls, using about 1 tablespoon for each. They do not need to be perfectly round. Once they are all formed, drop into boiling water. Reduce heat to medium-low, cover, and cook for 40 minutes. Using slotted spoon, transfer to serving bowl; cover to keep warm.

In another saucepan of boiling salted water, cook noodles (if serving) according to package directions. Drain and place in another serving bowl.

Place colander over soup tureen or serving bowl; strain broth into tureen. Place chicken on one platter, vegetables on another, and cover to keep warm. Serve bowls of soup at the stove, adding chicken, matzo balls or noodles, and vegetables as each person chooses.

Makes 10 to 12 servings.

Spring Goose Soup with Dumplings

This soothing meal in a bowl was submitted by the Netaweketata Food Security Committee of Fort Albany via Gigi Veeraraghavan, Fort Albany's healthy babies co-ordinator. Gigi and Joan Metatawabin have been voluntarily running the Fort Albany school nutrition program in the remote community on James Bay for over a decade. Gigi and Joan visited FoodShare's Field to Table Community Food Hub to work out the details of a pilot program in which FoodShare ships produce to Fort Albany in the winter months, when there is no road access. FoodShare is able to provide higher quality produce at better prices than any other southern supplier.

Canada Goose is a staple for the James Bay Cree. As the winter days lengthen, people prepare their blinds for the spring hunt. April is the month of the Goose Moon, when rivers and muskeg begin to thaw and the geese return to the North. "A-wuk, a-wuk!" calls everyone, from children to elders, to the geese flying overhead.

This is a simple recipe to celebrate the first spring goose, and dumplings make the soup even better. You can cook it over a camp fire or on your stovetop. Start making dumplings at least 20 minutes before you expect to eat.

1 whole goose (8–9 lb/3.5–4 kg), cleaned, skinned, cut in pieces

2 onions, chopped

3 stalks celery, cut in chunks

5 carrots, cut in chunks

5 Yukon Gold potatoes, cut in chunks

2½ tsp salt

Dumplings

1 cup flour

2 tsp baking powder

½ tsp salt

½ cup milk

Salt and freshly ground black pepper to taste

Place goose pieces in a large stock pot; add onions, celery, carrots, potatoes, salt, and water to cover. Bring to a boil. Reduce heat, partially cover, and simmer for 1 hour.

For dumplings, in medium bowl sift together flour, baking powder, and salt. Add milk; stir to make wet dough.

After soup has simmered for 40 minutes, drop in dumpling dough by tablespoons. Cover and let dumplings steam (do not lift lid) for 15 minutes. Season soup with salt and pepper.

Makes 6 to 8 servings.

Putting Food First:
Three Simple Actions for Personal, Collective, and Social Change

Despite the many problems surrounding food and our food system, great change can come from taking just a few actions in our own lives. Here are some simple but effective ways to take action.

IN OUR PERSONAL LIVES

- Eat 8 to 10 servings of fresh vegetables and fruits a day.
- Buy local, seasonal, fair-trade organic food.
- Sit down to at least one more home-cooked meal a week with friends and family.

AT THE COMMUNITY LEVEL

- Know where your food comes from by shopping at a farmers' market, through a food box program, or by joining a community shared agriculture (CSA) program.
- Get involved in a community garden, kitchen, or local student nutrition program.
- Create good soil by composting.

AT THE POLITICAL LEVEL

- Work with all three levels of government to create a cost-shared universal student nutrition program.
- Ask the federal government to ensure that Canada is food secure now and in the future and that all Canadians have adequate access to food by creating a ministry responsible for food security.
- Support Alternative Land Use Services (ALUS), which provide payments to farmers for environmental stewardship and to those such as schools, hospitals, and farmers' markets that use sustainable practices to grow food for local consumption.

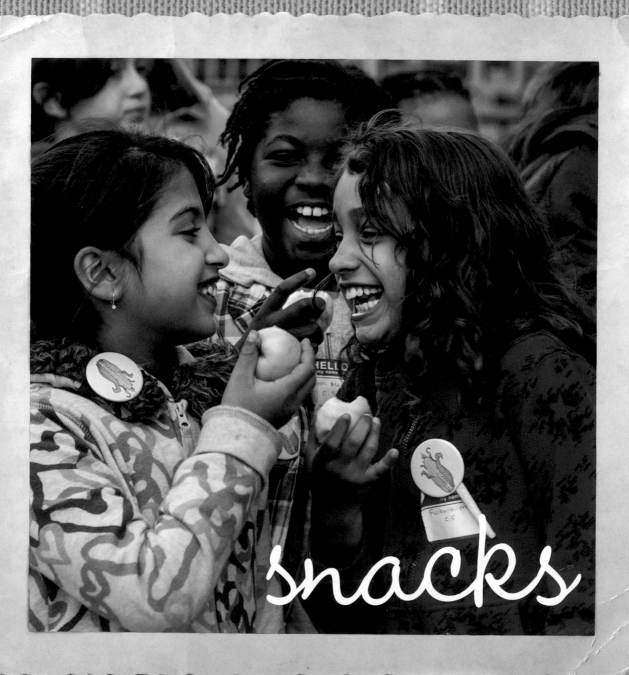

snacks

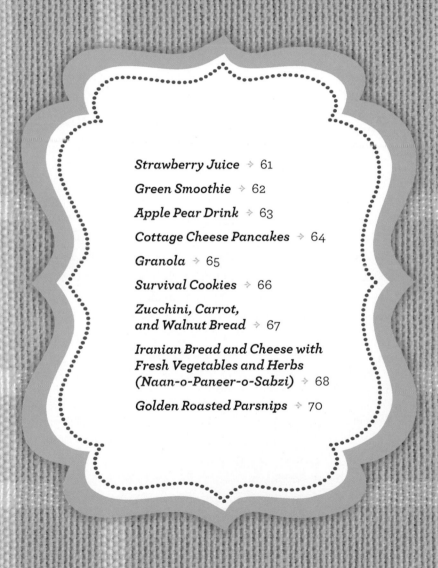

schools

Children love snacks, small items they can eat in a few bites. Most of us remember our childhood favourites and how much fun it was to eat many small meals when we were hungry instead of waiting for a big, formal meal. There are many reasons for adults to choose numerous small meals over fewer large ones, too.

FoodShare has been involved in creating healthier snacks at schools since 1985, when we worked to extend the Toronto District School Board's snack program to more schools. We are one of the pioneers of Toronto's student nutrition programs, and in partnership with school boards and Toronto Public Health provide the community development organizing for 700 universal student nutrition programs, in which 141,000 students enjoy healthy, culturally appropriate meals daily.

Our Fresh Produce for Schools and Community Agencies program delivers affordable bulk access to vegetables and fruit. The Field to Table Schools program works with educators, parents, and students, implementing hands-on cooking and gardening activities from JK through Grade 12 that support the curriculum with the goal of making Food Literacy a requirement of graduation. And our Good Food Café, which the *Toronto Star* called "the future of school lunches," provides a model for children choosing healthy foods in a cafeteria program.

In partnership with the school, we support Canada's first school-based market garden at Bendale Business and Technical Institute, where students plant, grow, and harvest vegetables on the school lawns and in the greenhouse, cook the food in culinary arts classes, and serve it in the cafeteria, proving that nutritious food and Food Literacy can be fully integrated into the school curriculum.

All these programs are together resulting in a massive movement of behavioural change as schools implement successful initiatives that FoodShare has pioneered. It is the only organization in North America providing a multifaceted approach to school food.

Adults are often hesitant to let children experiment with food. Brooke Ziebell, Field to Table Schools co-ordinator at FoodShare, finds in her work every day that "when you let children and young people choose what they want to eat, they will surprise you and try so many new things!" Ulla Knowles, a manager in our Student Nutrition program, also points to "the best kind of peer pressure," which she sees when children try new foods together in universal snack programs and learn that they enjoy them. We hope that you, too, will experiment with these delicious snacks for children of all ages and for any time of day.

Strawberry Juice

From Amanda Lipinski, diabetes prevention co-ordinator with the Southern Ontario Aboriginal Diabetes Initiative, comes this lovely drink, which she tells us is of special significance in Aboriginal communities: "Strawberries are an important medicine to Aboriginal people and are one of the first medicines that come to us after a long winter. Strawberry juice is an easy, refreshing, and healthy drink to nourish and hydrate our bodies and spirit."

Amanda loves to share this drink when she joins FoodShare in the community kitchens facilitated for Aboriginal parents by Leonard Abel, FoodShare's community kitchen educator. She says, "It is a joy to sit down in a school cafeteria with a large group of First Nations families, blessed by a community elder, participating in a healthy, delicious meal prepared by parents and students." Use fresh Ontario strawberries when in season.

4 cups strawberries, fresh if possible, thawed if frozen

6 cups water

½ cup maple syrup

Ice (optional)

Using food processor or blender, purée strawberries, water, and maple syrup until smooth. Divide among glasses and serve over ice (if using).

Makes 8 servings.

The strawberries in our boxes today are so good! Everyone loves them. Julia said they reminded her of the strawberries in her grandmother's garden when she was little, and she just couldn't stop smelling them. She had to open her box at once to try them and she licked off all the strawberry juice that ran down her arm.
COORDINATOR OF A GOOD FOOD BOX STOP

Green Smoothie

Carolynne Crawley, one of FoodShare's Field to Table Schools educators, has an unsurpassed passion for healthy eating and is a creative and motivational role model like no other. On any day, one can hear her booming voice as she sings the praises of all foods fresh and untainted. Students from 4 to 18 sit rapt in the teaching kitchen while Carolynne fills their heads with ideas and their stomachs with food that a lesser educator might struggle to get accepted. Everyone leaves her workshops with a new understanding of the joys and importance of good eating. What follows is Carolynne's signature smoothie, a surefire way to make sure youngsters and oldsters alike eat their greens.

1 pear, cored and quartered

1 very ripe banana

1 cup water

1 cup firmly packed kale, chard, or spinach leaves

1 or 2 pitted dried dates (optional)

1 cup crushed ice (optional)

Using food processor or blender, process all ingredients until smooth.

Makes 2 to 4 servings.

FoodShare is cooking up a Recipe for Change: reminding children what food is and where it comes from, teaching that healthy food also tastes good, and helping them to choose it for themselves. After many years of mapping curriculum connections to food and creating innovative workshops, tools, and resources for teachers, Recipe for Change takes our vision for students to new heights: a healthy cafeteria in every school and all students being taught to cook, garden, and compost throughout all the subject areas. FoodShare is leading the charge to embed food education in the Ontario curriculum and make Food Literacy a requirement of graduation for our students.

Apple Pear Drink

From Olivia Chow, member of parliament for Trinity-Spadina and a leading Canadian friend of food who tabled the first private member's bill on child and student nutrition. This drink comes from her mother, Ho Sze Chow, and is a treat that is also good for soothing the throat. Find north–south almonds at Chinese herbal medicine stores, where they are sometimes called bitter almonds. You can keep the cooked fruit in the drink or strain it and serve on the side as a compote.

12 north–south almonds

2 apples, cored and cut in large pieces

2 pears, cored and cut in large pieces

4 pitted dried dates

In saucepan, combine almonds and 4 cups water. Bring to a boil; boil for 10 minutes. Stir in apples, pears, and dates; return to a boil. Reduce heat to low and simmer uncovered about 35 minutes.

Serve hot or warm.

Makes about 4 servings.

Cottage Cheese Pancakes

Marion Kane's mother used to make this as a breakfast dish served with applesauce and yogurt for Marion's father. A great morning protein boost. Children of all ages love these and they make a perfect after-school snack or a light dinner when served with a salad and side vegetable dish. You could add a little wheat germ and/or some dried fruit to the batter if desired.

1 cup cottage cheese

2 eggs

¼ cup whole-wheat or all-purpose flour

¼ tsp cinnamon

Pinch salt

Place cottage cheese and eggs in food processor or blender; process until smooth. Transfer to bowl; stir in flour, cinnamon, and salt to form smooth, thick batter.

In lightly greased frying pan set over medium heat, drop batter by scant quarter cups. Cook 3 minutes or until bubbles appear on surface. Turn and cook about 2 minutes more until golden. You may have to reduce heat with successive batches to prevent pancakes from burning.

Makes about 8 pancakes.

Alice Waters' Edible Schoolyard, Debbie Field's Good Food Café, and the Bendale school farm show that children and young adults will actually eat good, healthy food as long as the emphasis is on the good.

JEANNIE MARSHALL, *Outside the Box: Why Our Children Need Real Food, Not Food Products*

Granola

A fantastic, nutrient-packed granola from Adrienne, who loves concocting and converting recipes to make them vegan. This one combines inspiration from many sources, including landmark cookbook How It All Vegan, *a trip to Maynooth, Ontario, and delicious meals shared there with political pioneers, plus a sunny visit to the town's wonderful farmers' market. Adrienne prepares this granola weekly as a breakfast staple, but you could take a small amount along for an excellent go-anywhere snack all on its own. Feel free to add some chopped dried apricots, figs, and/or prunes in place of or in addition to raisins and cranberries.*

3½ cups large-flake rolled oats

1 cup roughly chopped raw almonds (skin on)

½ cup barley flakes

½ cup kamut flakes

½ cup raw pumpkin seeds

½ cup spelt flakes

½ cup wheat bran

½ cup wheat germ

¼ cup ground almonds

¼ cup flax seeds

¼ cup sesame seeds

½ tsp salt

½ cup maple syrup

½ cup vegetable oil

¾ cup unsweetened finely shredded coconut

½ cup raisins

½ cup dried cranberries

Arrange oven racks with one in top third and other in bottom third of oven. Preheat oven to 350°F (180°C).

In large bowl, stir together oats, chopped almonds, barley flakes, kamut flakes, pumpkin seeds, spelt flakes, wheat bran, wheat germ, ground almonds, flax seeds, sesame seeds, and salt.

In small bowl, whisk together maple syrup and oil; stir into oat mixture until ingredients are evenly coated. Divide mixture between two large rimmed baking sheets.

Place both baking sheets in the oven. Bake for 10 minutes. Remove from oven, stir thoroughly and return to oven, switching pans from top to bottom. Bake another 8 minutes or until mixture is toasted. Stir in coconut, raisins, and cranberries. Cool on baking sheets. Store in air-tight containers.

Makes about 13 cups.

Survival Cookies

From former FoodShare urban agriculture intern Clare Giovannetti comes this fantastic cookie recipe, handed down through the family from her grandmother. Clare's mother uses 2½ cups chopped dried dates but Clare prefers to use 1¼ cup each dried apricots and cranberries. This makes a lot of big cookies; you will need to bake in several batches.

2 cups butter, softened

1½ cups packed light brown sugar

1¼ cups granulated sugar

3 eggs

1 tbsp vanilla extract

1¼ cups all-purpose flour

1¼ cups whole-wheat flour

1½ tsp baking soda

½ tsp salt

3¾ cups large-flake rolled oats

1½ cups raw unsalted sunflower seeds

1½ cups raw pumpkin seeds

1¼ cups chopped dried apricots

1¼ cups dried cranberries

¾ cup poppy seeds

Line several large rimmed baking sheets with parchment paper.

In bowl and using electric mixer (or in stand mixer and using paddle attachment), beat butter with sugars until creamy. One at a time, beat in eggs. Beat in vanilla.

In another bowl, stir together flours, baking soda, and salt; using wooden spoon, stir into butter mixture. Stir in oats, sunflower seeds, pumpkin seeds, apricots, cranberries, and poppy seeds.

Using ¼ cup measure or ice cream scoop, scoop dough onto prepared baking sheets, spacing 2 inches (5 cm) apart. Chill for 1 hour.

Preheat oven to 350°F (180°C).

One baking sheet at a time, bake in centre of oven for 15 to 18 minutes or until cooked through. Cool on baking sheet 5 minutes before transferring to wire rack to cool.

Makes about 40 large cookies.

Zucchini, Carrot, and Walnut Bread

The Regent Park Sole Support Mothers Group started Toronto's first community garden in the 1980s. Stuart Coles and Jennifer Welsh were inspired by this visionary group to ask the City of Toronto to start FoodShare in order to, among other things, "plant victory gardens everywhere" and expand community gardening. Three decades later, community gardening has become a broad social movement, growing food across the entire city.

Zucchini is a crop that can really take off, and it is a familiar experience to many gardeners to have a sudden, profuse harvest. To deal with this challenge creatively, many community gardeners develop zucchini recipes. This recipe comes from Norma Dickinson, a Toronto garden leader who worked with FoodShare to organize a process in which community gardens were located and counted city wide. That information was added to our FoodLink hotline, through which callers can find out how to access food and food programs in their neighbourhood. This bread is a tasty and healthy snack for children and adults alike.

1½ cups whole-wheat flour

1½ cups all-purpose flour

2 tsp cinnamon

2 tsp baking soda

2 tsp baking powder

1 tsp salt

2 eggs

1¾ cups brown sugar

½ cup vegetable oil

1 cup plain yogurt

1 tbsp vanilla extract

2 cups shredded zucchini

1 cup shredded carrots

1 cup chopped walnuts

Preheat oven to 350°F (180°C). Grease two 8- × 4-inch (1.5 L) loaf pans and set aside.

In small bowl, stir together flours, cinnamon, baking soda, baking powder, and salt.

In large bowl, beat eggs with sugar, oil, yogurt, and vanilla. Gently stir in flour mixture. Fold in zucchini, carrots, and walnuts until well combined, being careful not to over-mix.

Divide batter between the two prepared pans. Bake in centre of oven for 50 to 60 minutes or until tester inserted in centre comes out clean. Cool in pans on rack for 10 minutes. Turn out onto rack; cool completely.

(Tip: To bake muffins instead, divide batter between two paper-lined or greased 12-cup muffin tins and bake for 20 to 25 minutes.)

Makes 2 loaves or 24 muffins.

Iranian Bread and Cheese with Fresh Vegetables and Herbs (Naan-o-Paneer-o-Sabzi)

No Iranian table (sofreh) would be complete without this do-it-yourself snack, explained here by Zahra Parvinian, FoodShare's director of social enterprise. Zahra's experience as a social worker and long-time co-ordinator of the Focus on Food youth internship program, along with her business training in Iran, allows her to balance the complex needs of one of the most successful food social enterprises in Canada. An efficient non-profit subsidized business, the Good Food program has annual sales of $1.75 million and is deeply committed to food access for low-income and immigrant communities. In running the program, Zahra brings her deep intuition about food to the table every day. The fundamental role that food plays in celebration is evidenced in this classic dish, which is a delight to share.

½ **bunch each: flat-leaf parsley, coriander, watercress, tarragon, mint, basil**

1 **bunch green onions, tops trimmed and discarded**

1 **bunch radishes, greens removed, cut in half**

1 **lb (500 g) feta cheese**

1 **cup each: almonds and walnut halves, soaked in water for 1 hour, drained and dried**

1 **large Iranian or Middle Eastern flat bread**

On large serving platter, arrange the herbs with whole green onions and radishes. Cut feta into slices and lay across middle of platter with a pile of almonds and walnuts on either side.

To eat, tear a piece of flat bread, top with feta, a few herbs, some radish, onion, and nuts. Fold up and enjoy. Nush-e jan!

Makes 8 servings.

Golden Roasted Parsnips

This recipe developed for FoodShare's school programs by Miriam Streiman of Mad Maple Farm, a country inn and agriturismo, showcases the earthy, sweet flavour of parsnips, making the dish popular even among those who don't normally choose root vegetables. Sixty enthusiastic Grade 4 students counted these as a highlight of the day at FoodShare's Eat-In Ontario, a fall harvest celebration for 600 students from JK to Grade 12 on the lawn of Queen's Park. Their taste buds were pleasantly surprised as they devoured this carrot cousin they had never tasted before.

Miriam, Joshna Maharaj, Katie Compton, and Carole Ferrari work with FoodShare to develop creative mid-morning snacks made from Ontario produce that are easy for student nutrition program co-ordinators to make. Our parsnips are grown by Mark Trealout and Laura Boyd of Grassroot Organics, a non-certified organic mixed farm practising sustainable agriculture techniques in the Kawarthas.

Golden and caramelized, these parsnips can be served as a side dish accompanying a hearty meal, puréed into a soup, chopped up in a salad, or served as is, just as the Grade 4 students enjoyed them.

6 parsnips, tops trimmed, quartered lengthwise

1 tbsp olive oil

1 tsp maple syrup

½ tsp each: salt and freshly ground black pepper

¼ tsp red chili flakes (optional)

1 tbsp unsalted butter, softened

Preheat oven to 400°F (200°C). Line a rimmed baking sheet with parchment paper.

In medium bowl, combine parsnips, oil, maple syrup, salt, pepper, and chili flakes. Toss to coat and spread evenly on prepared tray. Dot parsnips with small knobs of butter.

Place in oven, roast until golden and slightly tender, 25 to 30 minutes. Rotate tray halfway through roasting.

Makes 4 servings.

I think I now have at least some idea of what a stampede sounds like: it sounds like sixty grade 7 and 8 students stomping down a flight of stairs, then running along the basement concrete-block hallway of a big old school in order to get to the cafeteria. I remember what that teenage hunger felt like. What I don't remember is good, healthy, home-cooked food at the end of the hallway sprint. These students, though—most running at full tilt, some skipping, one timing her steps to a chant of "quick, quick" said to no one in particular—are racing toward a meal that is one part lunch and one part radical (and radically simple) experiment: "We're proving that kids will eat good, healthy, nutritious home-cooked meals full of fresh fruits and vegetables," says Debbie Field, executive director of FoodShare.

LORRAINE JOHNSTON, WRITING IN *City Farmer: Adventures in Urban Food Growing* ON THE GOOD FOOD CAFÉ

starters and sides

community development

It is often said that Toronto is one of the most diverse cities in the world, and perhaps one of the most profound experiments in racial and social harmony anywhere. Visit schools across the city and you will hear more than 80 languages spoken, and see children playing together from cultures that might have been fighting in their parents' home countries. There is an openness to diversity and complexity in Toronto, whether in sexual orientation, gender, ability, language, or culture. We have a sense here that we live side by each, and that each side of the discussion is relevant. Openness to diversity is an integral part of FoodShare's work. We believe we are strengthened by our many voices and experiences, and promote working together beyond barriers to build a new food system that fundamentally respects diversity of all kinds.

FoodShare recognizes that long-term systemic change can happen only when we work together, creating solutions that build on the energy and strengths of many. For almost 30 years we have worked in social housing buildings and with tenant associations and community leaders in neighbourhoods across the city to develop food programs. We partner in many of Toronto's communities to build on existing strengths and knowledge to develop and grow solutions.

FoodShare's community food animators work side by side with neighbourhood leaders and community organizations to help them meet their own food needs and create healthy futures, bringing food to life with Good Food Markets and community gardens and kitchens. We share all our resources, inviting groups and communities to adapt our programs so that they work in diverse neighbour-hoods and contexts.

In honouring the many cultures of Toronto, we have learned from our partners that local cannot be the only criterion in choosing food. As Anan Lololi, executive director of the Afri-Can Food Basket, taught us in his comments at a June 2000 Farmers' Markets Ontario meeting at FoodShare, "I will come to the farmers' market to buy an apple, but I need you to sell me a mango, too."

So from diverse kitchens and communities across our city to your kitchen, here is a medley of delicious sides to delight and expand your global repertoire.

Guacamole

FoodShare's Kitchen Incubator program provides entrepreneurs with a fully outfitted and certified co-operative kitchen from which to launch their food companies, and has introduced FoodShare to many fine chefs, among them Claudia Huerta from El Cilantro Catering. Claudia is a marvellous cook whose food can be eaten at many Toronto festivals throughout the summer months.

In her list of helpful hints for this classic guacamole, she stresses the need for the right ingredients: "When you buy your avocados, get them green and ripen them at home. Use only fresh green chilies; use firm, ripe tomatoes, with little or no juice. These are ingredients I never use in my guacamole: lime (it helps with the oxidation and preserves the guacamole but it changes the flavour), mayonnaise, and sour cream. They have never been used in guacamole in Mexico."

Claudia's guacamole is a simple, fresh dish that is delicious because of the care taken with ingredients and process. Serve with yellow corn tortilla chips. Buen provecho!

2 large ripe Hass avocados

Salt to taste

1 jalapeño, serrano, or Jamaican chili, finely chopped

1 small tomato, chopped (about ½ cup)

1 small onion, finely chopped (about ¼ cup)

2 tbsp chopped fresh coriander

Cut avocados in half; remove and discard the large pits. Scoop out flesh with a metal spoon and place in medium bowl. Add salt and chopped chili. Mash the avocado mixture with a potato masher or the back of a fork until creamy, with few lumps.

Add tomato, onion, and coriander; stir to combine.

Makes about 4 servings.

White Bean Slather with Caramelized Onions and Goat Cheese

This fantastic vegetarian dish sent to us by Alberta food writer Cinda Chavich can be spread on toasted baguette slices with soup or salad for a light meal. It also makes a great appetizer. Try with sweet onions such as Vidalia or Honey Sweet.

¼ cup olive oil

2 cups thinly sliced onion

½ cup combination of chopped fresh rosemary, sage, and thyme

2 cloves garlic, finely chopped

1 tsp balsamic vinegar

Dash hot pepper sauce

1 can (19 oz/540 mL) white kidney beans, rinsed and drained

3 tbsp olive oil

Salt and freshly ground black pepper to taste

4 oz (125 g) soft goat cheese, crumbled

In large frying pan, heat ¼ cup oil over medium-low heat. Add onions; cook, stirring often, until soft and golden brown, about 40 minutes.

Meanwhile, place herbs, garlic, vinegar, and hot sauce in food processor; pulse on and off to combine. Add half the beans and 1½ tablespoons of oil; process until smooth. Add remaining beans and oil; pulse on and off until all ingredients are combined but still chunky.

When onions are golden, stir bean mixture into frying pan. Heat through. Add salt and pepper. Sprinkle with goat cheese; toss together lightly and remove from heat. The cheese should be melting but still visible in small pieces.

Serve warm or at room temperature.

Makes 2 cups (about 6 servings).

Onion Bhajia with Tamarind Sauce

Recipe for Change is FoodShare's annual signature event to raise funds and consciousness about our work in schools. The Torontoist website called Recipe for Change "a Food Network fantasy come to life," James Chatto called it "a must attend," and the National Post said it was "the perfect foodie fundraiser." The event includes a lovely meal and accompanying beverages, prepared by 30 top Toronto chefs, among them Abby Sabherwal of Magical Catering, who shares this recipe. Born in India, schooled in nutrition, and inspired by the cooking of her mother and grandmothers, Abby makes all natural food that reflects their love and affection.

This recipe makes 2 cups of sauce. Keep what you do not immediately eat with your bhajia refrigerated in a sealed jar for up to 2 months.

Bhajia

1 cup besan (chickpea flour)

2 tbsp ground cumin

1 tsp salt

2 tsp seeded, chopped jalapeño

2 cups thinly sliced sweet onion

1 cup vegetable oil, for frying

Tamarind Sauce

½ lb (250g) seeded tamarind

2 cups boiling water

1 cup granulated sugar

2 tbsp roasted ground
        cumin seeds

1 tbsp salt

1 tsp each: chili powder and
        freshly ground black
        pepper

½ tsp ground ginger

For bhajia batter, put besan, cumin, salt, jalapeño, and ⅔ cup cold water in food processor or blender; process on high for 2 to 3 minutes. This will incorporate air into the batter to make it fluffy. Set aside to rest for 30 minutes at room temperature.

For sauce, break tamarind into small pieces, place in a medium bowl and cover with boiling water. Let sit for one hour. Mash and strain over another bowl, pressing the tamarind into the strainer so that all the smooth pulp comes out. Discard contents of strainer. Add sugar to pulp, mix until dissolved. Stir in cumin seeds, salt, chili powder, pepper, and ginger.

To cook bhajia, in medium frying pan heat oil to 375°F (190°C). Gather a small handful of onion rings (about ¼ cup) and dip into the batter to coat completely. Drop immediately into the hot oil and fry until golden brown, turning if necessary to brown both sides. Remove with a slotted spoon and transfer to paper towel–lined plate to drain. Repeat with remaining onions.

Serve bhajia with tamarind sauce.

Makes 4 servings.

Lee Landsberg's Latkes

Visionary Toronto journalist, activist, and author Michele Landsberg contributed her mother Lee's recipe for these wonderful Jewish potato pancakes. She tells us, "My mother was a dainty little beauty with a brilliant gift for light cooking. Her latkes are the world's best and I am sharing them only because it is FoodShare!" We call the recipe Lee Landsberg's Latkes so her name (and skill) will live on.

These are small latkes; make them bigger if desired. They turn out more rounded than your average latke; feel free to shape them with your hands instead of a spoon for the more conventional version. Michele warns, "All specifics (peanut oil, russet potatoes) are there for a reason, and results cannot be guaranteed if there are substitutes."

Peanut oil

4 large baking (russet) potatoes, peeled and each cut in 8 pieces

2 onions, cut in chunks

2 eggs, separated

4 tsp potato flour or all-purpose flour

1 tsp baking powder

1 tsp salt

1 tsp granulated sugar

Place large colander in sink; line with clean tea towel. (Do not use terry cloth type.)

Pour 1 inch (2.5 cm) oil into deep frying pan or electric frying pan; start heating to 400°F (200°C).

Place half the potatoes and onions in blender; add enough cold water to cover, about 3 cups. Pulse mixture until vegetables are ground to size of rice grains. Pour into prepared colander; drain. Gather ends of tea towel into bundle and squeeze out all the water you can, being careful potato mush doesn't squish out the top. Mixture should be crumbly and moist, not wet. Place in large bowl. Repeat with remaining potatoes and onions.

In small bowl, beat egg yolks lightly. Beat in potato flour, baking powder, salt, and sugar. Stir into potato mixture.

In another bowl and using electric mixer, beat egg whites until stiff peaks form. Using spatula, gently fold into potato mixture until well blended. Drop mixture by rounded tablespoons into hot oil and lightly tap the top of each one with back of spoon to make it a bit flatter. Fry in batches until crisp and golden around edges, then turn to fry other side, about 1½ minutes per side. Do not overcrowd the pan. Drain on paper towel. Between batches, scoop out and discard any brown floating scraps and make sure the oil returns to 400°F (200°C). Top up oil as needed to maintain depth of 1 inch (2.5 cm).

Serve with applesauce and sour cream.

Makes about 6 servings.

Garlic and callaloo, when planted, multiply the next season—where there is one clove, the next year will be six; when you plant one seed of callaloo, the next year there will be hundreds. Where there is one food initiative, there are quickly more. Where there is a Good Food Market, there is a Community Kitchen. Where there is a Community Garden, there is a Good Food Market.
FOODSHARE'S ANGELA ELZINGACHENG IN A CITY OF TORONTO VIDEO PROFILING SOME OF OUR WORK

*share * starters and sides*

79

Salt Cod Fritters with Garlic Mayonnaise

From Deborah Reid, a talented Toronto chef, comes this versatile dish. Salt cod can be bought bone in or boneless. It's easier to use the boneless kind for this dish. Serve 3 or 4 fritters as a light meal with salad and bread or as a delectable hors d'oeuvre. A potato ricer can be found in most cookware stores.

Fritters

1 lb (500 g) boneless skinless salt cod

2 lb (1 kg) Yukon Gold potatoes

4 cloves garlic, finely chopped

1 tbsp finely chopped fresh parsley

4 egg yolks

Salt and freshly ground black pepper
    to taste

Vegetable oil

½ cup fine dry breadcrumbs

Garlic Mayonnaise

1 cup mayonnaise

1 large clove garlic, finely chopped

2 tsp white wine vinegar

Salt and freshly ground black pepper
    to taste

Place salt cod in baking dish. Add cold water to cover. Cover dish and refrigerate for 3 days, changing water daily.

Cut potatoes in half or, if very large, in quarters. Place drained salt cod and potatoes in large saucepan. Add cold water to cover. Bring to a boil; cook until potatoes are tender when pierced with tip of sharp knife, about 12 minutes. Drain.

As soon as potatoes are cool enough to handle, peel them. Put warm potatoes through a ricer into bowl. Crumble salt cod into riced potatoes. Stir in garlic, parsley and egg yolks. Add salt and pepper, being careful not to over-season as salt cod is salty.

Shape mixture into small balls, using about 2 teaspoons for each. Place on rimmed baking sheet as you shape them. (Make ahead: You can store covered in the fridge in a single layer up to 24 hours before frying.)

For garlic mayonnaise, in bowl, whisk together mayonnaise, garlic, vinegar, and 2 tablespoons water. Add salt and pepper. Cover and chill until serving.

Heat oil in deep fryer to 375°F (190°C).

Place breadcrumbs in shallow bowl. In batches, lightly dredge cod balls in breadcrumbs and fry for about 2 minutes or until golden. Drain on paper towel. Best served immediately.

Serve with garlic mayonnaise as a dip.

Makes about 8 dozen small fritters.

Skillet Cornbread

From Cynthia Peters, cookbook author, personal chef, chair of FoodShare's advisory council, and owner of From the Farm Cooking School, comes this sensational cornbread. Serve with hot pepper jelly. If you don't like the taste of darkly caramelized onion, stir the cooked onions into the batter before baking or simply omit them. Cynthia recommends adding other vegetables such as mushrooms, peppers, or zucchini at the onion-cooking stage for a twist that gives more texture.

1 tbsp vegetable oil

1 small onion, finely chopped

1½ cups cornmeal

½ cup all-purpose flour

2 tsp baking powder

1 tsp salt

1½ cups buttermilk

3 eggs, lightly beaten

⅓ cup unsalted butter, melted

1 tbsp liquid honey

1 cup fresh, frozen, or canned and drained corn kernels

¼ cup chopped fresh chives or green onions

Preheat oven to 425°F (220°C).

In 10-inch (25 cm) cast-iron or other oven-proof frying pan, heat oil over medium heat. Swirl pan to ensure sides are coated in oil. Add onions; cook for 5 minutes or until soft.

Meanwhile, in bowl, stir together cornmeal, flour, baking powder, and salt.

In another bowl, stir together buttermilk, eggs, butter, and honey; pour over dry ingredients and stir just until moistened. Stir in corn and chives.

Pour batter into hot frying pan on top of onions. Bake in centre of oven for 30 minutes or until golden on top and tester inserted in centre comes out clean.

Cut into wedges. Serve warm with butter or red pepper jelly.

Makes 1 loaf.

Baked Bannock

Bannock, or fry bread, is a food staple in the Aboriginal tradition. Leonard Abel, a member of the FoodShare kitchen team and a community kitchen educator, created this baked version. Since we started preparing it in our First Nations community kitchens, it has become a favourite that is served at gatherings from sunrise ceremonies to solstice celebrations.

5 cups all-purpose flour (or try ½ whole-wheat flour)

¼ tsp salt

4 tbsp baking powder

½ cup dried cranberries

⅓ cup melted butter

Preheat oven to 350°F (180°C).

In large bowl, combine flour, salt, baking powder, and cranberries. Pour melted butter and 2½ cups water over mixture; stir with fork to form dough into a ball.

Turn onto a floured surface and knead gently about 10 times. Pat into a flat disc about 1 inch (2.5 cm) thick. Bake in middle of oven on a greased rimmed baking sheet for 25 to 30 minutes, until lightly browned.

Makes 1 loaf.

We have always found FoodShare to be very generous with sharing information, resources, ideas. The sharing of resources such as the Salad Bar manual, the Gardening manual, Making Homemade Baby Food, and others has helped our small organization develop programs that have been helpful for low-income families and neighbourhoods. We were able to be much more effective as we were able to avoid mistakes that first-time programs incur. FoodShare supports learning circles across the country.

KAREN ARCHIBALD, CHILD HUNGER AND
EDUCATION PROGRAM, SASKATOON

Farinata

FoodShare board member Aruna Handa shares this kid-friendly side dish, a crepe made from chickpea flour. Dr. Handa writes and lectures about philosophy and food, and currently, with Mike Paduada, is convening the Centre for Social Innovation (CSI) Annex Food Constellation, a group dedicated to building capacity in the good food sector.

Farinata has a venerable history and is so tasty that many cultures have developed their own version, with names such as socca *in Nice and* faina *in Uruguay and Argentina. Farinata is similar to focaccia and can be made into a pizza, eaten plain, or topped with cheese, pesto, or rosemary. It is a brilliant snack food and perfect for those who cannot eat wheat, particularly in pasta-eating regions where avoiding gluten can be a real challenge. It is surprisingly easy to make and a real delight.*

⅔ **cup besan (chickpea flour)**

½ **tsp salt**

¼ **cup olive oil**

¼ **cup chopped fresh herbs (e.g., rosemary, oregano, thyme)**

Freshly ground black pepper to taste

In medium bowl, whisk together besan, salt, 1 cup water, and 1 tablespoon oil until smooth. Cover and set aside for 30 minutes.

Preheat oven to 375°F (190°C).

Heat a medium cast-iron frying pan (or other oven-proof pan) to medium-high. Add 1 tablespoon oil and move the pan around to coat the bottom and halfway up the sides of the pan. Pour one-third of the batter into the pan, swirling to cover the bottom completely; sprinkle with one-third of the herbs and a good pinch pepper.

Place frying pan in oven and bake on middle rack for 8 minutes or until the batter starts to pull away from the edges of the pan. Remove farinata from the pan with a flat metal spatula, place on large plate, and set aside. Repeat the baking process twice more with remaining batter.

Serve warm or at room temperature.

Makes 3 to 6 servings.

Cucumber Raita

This dish comes from FoodShare board member Hélène St. Jacques and her neighbour Georgia Nayar. It is from their self-published cookbook, Indian Cooking with Georgia. *Georgia grew up in a home of Greek heritage and cooking traditions. She learned to cook Indian food when she married into an Indian family. Georgia's raita is the perfect complement to many of the dishes in this book, as it's cool, refreshing, and soothing to the palate. It is also an ideal salad or side dish to serve children. Cucumbers are a Good Food Café favourite, and raita, with its creamy sweetness, is a surefire kid pleaser.*

1 English cucumber
½ tsp salt
2 cups plain yogurt
¼ tsp cayenne pepper
1 tsp cumin seeds, toasted
1 tbsp fresh mint, chopped

Shred cucumber. Place in mesh strainer with salt; stir together and squeeze to drain out water.

In medium bowl, mix drained cucumber with yogurt. Stir in cayenne and toasted cumin seeds. Chill.

To serve, sprinkle with mint.

Makes 3 cups.

Oven-Baked Mushrooms (Funghi al Forno)

This brilliant recipe is from Eugenia Barato, chef/owner of Trattoria Giancarlo in Toronto's Little Italy. Serve with crusty bread to mop up the juices, as either an appetizer or a side dish with roast meat, fish, or poultry. Reduce the hot pepper flakes, if desired. Eugenia likes to use Parmigiano Reggiano.

⅓ cup chopped fresh parsley

6 cloves garlic, finely chopped

1 tsp hot pepper flakes

1½ lb (750 g) assorted mushrooms (e.g., shiitake, oyster, brown)

½ cup olive oil

2 tbsp balsamic vinegar

½ tsp salt

1½ cups grated Parmesan cheese

Preheat oven to 400°F (200°C).

In small bowl, stir together parsley, garlic, and hot pepper flakes.

Trim mushroom stems and brush off any dirt with damp cloth. Discard shiitake stems.

In large bowl, whisk together oil, vinegar, and salt. Add mushrooms; toss to coat. Spread mushrooms in single layer on large rimmed baking sheet. Sprinkle with parsley mixture and Parmesan.

Bake in oven for 10 minutes or just until tender. Place mushrooms with juices on serving platter.

Makes about 6 servings.

Slow-Roasted Tomatoes

Lisa Kates, Toronto chef and firm believer in the idea that food brings people together, shares her recipe for roasted tomatoes. Lisa is deeply disturbed at the poor quality of food in Toronto's high schools and is working with other parents to get healthy, appealing food, like this wonderfully simple dish, into school cafeterias.

Community gardeners—those who use the hundreds of neighbourhood plots FoodShare helps bring to life and many more across the city—will rejoice at this use of their sweet, sunshine-infused harvest. You may want to roast the tomatoes a little longer to get the taste and texture you like. Use these as a pizza topping, in a sandwich or salad, or tossed with pasta. To make into a sauce, place warm tomatoes in a bowl and stir with ½ cup basil leaves torn into bite-sized pieces until tomatoes melt. Season to taste with salt and pepper. You could easily double or triple this recipe, especially in tomato season.

12 plum tomatoes
¼ cup olive oil
3 cloves garlic, sliced

Preheat oven to 250°F (120°C). Line large rimmed baking sheet with parchment paper.

Quarter tomatoes lengthwise. Place in single layer on prepared baking sheet. Drizzle with oil. Scatter garlic on and around tomatoes.

Roast in centre of oven, stirring occasionally, for 5 hours or until tomatoes are very soft, shrivelled, and charred at edges.

Makes about 1¾ cups.

Kenyan Kale (Sukuma Wiki)

Mwangi Wa Wairumu, a friend from Kenya, shares this wonderful recipe that we make at FoodShare on a weekly basis. Sukuma Wiki means extending the week. Kale is what people in his village eat when there's no chicken or meat left in the kitchen and an alternative is required. It's simple to prepare, delicious, and very good for you. In Ontario, kale extends the season as well as the week, as it is one of numerous crops that grow well in the fall. Along with carrots and Brussels sprouts it is frost tolerant. Kale's flavour actually improves with the frost and it is always amazing to see dark green kale with snow all around it.

1 tbsp vegetable oil

2 cloves garlic, finely chopped

1 onion, diced

1 large bunch kale, tough stems and ribs removed, chopped

3 tomatoes, diced, or 1½ cups canned diced tomatoes, drained

Salt and freshly ground black pepper to taste

Juice of 1 lemon (about 3–4 tbsp)

In large frying pan, sauté garlic in oil until fragrant, about 2 minutes, being careful not to let it burn. Add onion and continue cooking until transparent, another 3–4 minutes.

Add kale, tomatoes, salt, and pepper and continue cooking until the kale wilts but maintains its vibrant colour. Sprinkle with fresh lemon juice, toss and serve immediately.

Makes 4 to 6 servings.

This is exactly right! This is what we eat!

IMMACULATE TUMWINE, EXCITED TO FIND KALE IN HER GOOD FOOD BOX AND A RECIPE TO COOK IT JUST THE WAY THEY MAKE SUKUMA AT HOME IN UGANDA.

Ratatouille

Marion Kane perfected this excellent Provençal dish after several tries. Cut vegetables into ½- to 1-inch (1–2.5 cm) cubes. Cooking each vegetable separately before baking is the secret to success. This is great sprinkled with crumbled goat cheese or grated Gruyère and browned under the broiler before serving.

6 tbsp olive oil

4 zucchini, quartered lengthwise and cut in cubes

¼ tsp salt

1 sweet yellow pepper, cut in cubes

1 sweet red pepper, cut in cubes

1 large eggplant or 6 Japanese eggplants (skin on), cut in cubes

½ tsp salt

¼ tsp freshly ground black pepper

1 large red onion, cut in cubes

2 large cloves garlic, finely chopped

1 tbsp chopped fresh thyme, oregano, or herbes de Provence or 1 tsp dried

3 tomatoes, peeled, seeded, coarsely chopped

Preheat oven to 350°F (180°C).

In large frying pan, heat 1 tablespoon of the oil over medium-high heat. Add zucchini; sprinkle with ¼ teaspoon salt. Cook, stirring occasionally, for 5 minutes or until golden. Transfer to 20-cup (5 L) Dutch oven or casserole dish with lid.

Heat 1 tablespoon of the oil in same frying pan over medium-high heat. Add peppers; cook for 5 minutes, stirring occasionally. Add to zucchini.

Heat 3 tablespoons of the oil in frying pan over medium-high heat. Add eggplant; cook, stirring occasionally, for 5 minutes or until browned and slightly softened. Sprinkle with remaining salt and pepper. Stir into zucchini mixture.

Heat remaining tablespoon oil in frying pan over medium heat. Add onion, garlic, and thyme. Cook, stirring, for 4 minutes or until softened. Add tomatoes. Cover and cook about 10 minutes or until tomatoes form a sauce. You may have to add a little water. Season with salt and pepper. Pour over vegetables in Dutch oven but do not stir.

Cover and bake in oven for 20 minutes. Uncover. Cook 15 minutes more or until vegetables are tender but not mushy.

Serve warm, at room temperature, or chilled.

Makes 4 to 6 servings.

Brazilian Rice and Beans with Collard Greens (Arroz e Feijão com Couve à Mineira)

Cecilia Rocha and her sister, Bernadete Nobrega, share this Brazilian staple of rice, beans, and collard greens, which are made separately and served side by side on the same plate. In 1997, FoodShare executive director Debbie Field was introduced to the most advanced government-initiated food security programs while visiting Belo Horizonte, Brazil. Cecilia is a professor at the Ryerson Centre for Studies in Food Security and has become the English-language expert on Belo initiatives, writing on the successful Popular Restaurants program, subsidized-produce Sacolão Markets, and universal school food programs.

Like many around the world, Brazilians eat their larger meal in the middle of the day and a lighter meal such as this with fruit in the evening. You could serve it to accompany traditional Brazilian meat dishes or with a fresh salsa. Vegetarians will find this a colourful and nutritious complete meal.

Beans (Feijão)

1 cup dried beans (kidney, black, or pinto)
1 tbsp olive oil
1 clove garlic, finely chopped
Salt to taste
Juice of 1 lime (optional)

Rice (Arroz)

1 tbsp olive oil
3 cloves garlic, finely chopped
1 cup long-grain rice, rinsed and drained
1½ cups boiling water
1 tsp salt

Collard Greens (Couve à Mineira)

5 cloves garlic
1½ tsp salt
2 tbsp olive oil
2 large bunches collard greens, stems removed, leaves rolled into bundles and chopped
Freshly ground black pepper to taste

In large bowl, cover beans with water and soak overnight. Drain and boil in 4 cups water for 45 minutes or until tender. Drain.

In medium saucepan, heat oil. Add garlic and sauté for 1 minute. Add beans; cook for 5 minutes. Season with salt and lime juice (if using).

For rice, in medium saucepan sauté garlic in oil on medium heat. Add rice; toast for 2 to 3 minutes. Add boiling water and salt and return to boil. Reduce heat, cover, and simmer for 12 minutes. Remove from heat and rest, covered, for 10 minutes. Fluff with a fork.

For greens, finely chop garlic on a cutting board; add salt and mash into garlic with side of knife to make a paste. In large frying pan, heat oil over medium heat. Add the garlic paste and cook for 30 seconds. Add collard greens and sauté for 3 to 4 minutes or until leaves begin to soften and colour is bright green. Season with pepper.

To serve, place collard greens, beans, and rice side by side on a plate.

Makes 4 servings.

Red Lentil Sauce (Timtimo)

This recipe comes from Luam Kidane, co-ordinator of FoodShare's Focus on Food youth intern program. Luam, who is from Eritrea, roots her work in an anti-oppressive framework that facilitates an exchange of knowledge between her and the participants; the young people help her to learn as much as she helps them. Luam believes that the path to finding employment for young people cannot be found without recognizing and working to eliminate the explicit and implicit systemic barriers faced by black, racialized, and indigenous young people.

Timtimo is a popular dish throughout the Horn of Africa because it is inexpensive, nutritious, and very good to eat. It can be served as part of a fuller meal, as a dip replacing hummus, or in a sandwich.

¼ cup olive oil

1 onion, finely chopped

4 cloves garlic, crushed

2 jalapeños, seeded and chopped

1 cup diced tomato

2 tsp fresh dill, chopped

¼ tsp turmeric

1 cup cooked red lentils or about ½ can (19 oz/540mL), rinsed and drained

Salt to taste

In medium frying pan, heat oil to medium. Sauté onion, garlic, and jalapeños for 5 minutes. Add tomato, dill, and turmeric. Reduce heat, cover, and simmer for about 20 minutes. Add lentils and simmer for another 15 minutes. Add salt.

Serve on injera (Eritrean bread).

Makes 2 servings.

Matar Paneer

From fresh food enthusiast and blogger Charmian Christie comes this rich-tasting Indian vegetarian dish, which she created as a thank you to a helpful friend who loved matar paneer but couldn't afford to take the whole family out every time she craved it. This is now a go-to dinner in cold weather. Paneer is a fresh cheese common in South Asian cooking. Find it at Indian grocers or some specialty cheese shops.

¼ cup vegetable oil

2 large onions, finely chopped

2 tbsp grated or pressed garlic

2 tbsp grated ginger root

2 tbsp tomato paste

1 tbsp cumin seeds

1 tbsp garam masala

1 tbsp brown sugar

1 tsp hot pepper flakes, or to taste

½ tsp turmeric

1 tsp salt

5 oz (150 g) paneer, cut in cubes
 (1 cup)

2 cups fresh or frozen peas

½ cup plain yogurt

½ cup 10% cream

In non-stick frying pan, heat oil over medium-high heat. Cook onions until dark golden brown, stirring occasionally, about 10 to 15 minutes. Stir in garlic and ginger; reduce heat to medium and cook for 2 minutes. Stir in tomato paste and cumin seeds; cook, stirring, for 30 seconds. Reduce heat to low.

Stir in garam masala, brown sugar, hot pepper flakes, turmeric, and salt; cook for 5 minutes, stirring occasionally. Stir in paneer; cook for 5 minutes. Stir in peas, yogurt, and cream; cook for 2 to 4 minutes or until peas are just cooked through.

Serve immediately, sprinkled with fresh coriander, if desired.

Makes about 4 servings.

mains

fresh produce

When Mary Lou Morgan and Ursula Lipski began what they called the Field to Table program (the precursor to the Good Food program) at FoodShare in 1992, they articulated the deeply felt desire of many to create more direct links between farmers and consumers, particularly urban consumers. It has been great to see the term *field to table* become an adjective, representing the new distribution system that has developed over the past 20 years. Now when we shop for the food to go into our dinner, we can more readily get access to local food, sometimes even knowing the name of the farmer who grew it.

FoodShare's Good Food program connects families and communities with affordable, culturally diverse fresh vegetables and fruit. It builds communities; increases the consumption of healthy produce; and improves the income of small family farms. The Good Food Box delivers top-quality fresh produce through 200 volunteer-run drop-offs at which neighbours meet and form communities. Customers pay the cost of the produce itself, starting at just $13, while distribution is subsidized. We deliver about 50,000 bountiful boxes every year, serving 7,000 families and saving them an average of $9 per month.

FoodShare provides training and produce to support the operation of 17 Good Food Markets run by local groups in food deserts, where healthy fresh food is not otherwise available. These vibrant markets make available the same top-quality fruits and vegetables as the Good Food Box but allow shoppers to purchase in quantities that meet their cash flow needs, at the same time creating lively public spaces and breaking down social isolation.

FoodShare's Fresh Produce for Schools and Community Agencies program delivers produce directly to 250 schools, child care centres, and community agencies, serving 67,000 children every week. Our Field to Table Community Food Hub, with support from the Ontario government, is now also working to develop a distribution system that will ensure that public institutions such as schools can buy quality Ontario produce for food programs, further increasing the market for our farmers.

Torrie Warner of Warners Farm in Beamsville, Ontario, describes the mutual benefits of the new food system being created by FoodShare in partnership with local, organic, and Local Food Plus farmers: "I get to sell my fruit and FoodShare gets to distribute fresh local fruit. Good for the farmer, good for FoodShare, and good for the consumer. Win–win for all." And so from the abundance of Ontario farms to your kitchen, here are win–win main courses for every taste.

Rustic Bean Stew

From FoodShare chef and kitchen manager Alvin Rebick comes this homey and colourful vegan main dish. This recipe first appeared in the cookbook Bistro: Trade Secrets from a Life in Food, *by Alvin and Glenna Rebick, who also published* Very Best of the Baker Street Bistro. *Alvin and Glenna are an inspiring example of teamwork in the kitchen, having managed six restaurants, written two books, and raised two children together. Now they share their many years of food experience through teaching: Glenna through George Brown College and Alvin in all his work at FoodShare. This recipe is a testament to the healthy lunches shared daily at FoodShare by staff, volunteers, partners, and friends.*

¼ cup olive oil

2 cups sliced carrots

1 large onion, chopped

2 cloves garlic, finely chopped

1 tbsp dried tarragon

1 tsp dry mustard

1 tsp dried thyme

½ tsp cayenne pepper

2 sweet peppers (red, yellow, orange, or a combination), coarsely chopped

2 cups (about 5 oz/150 g) quartered mushrooms

3 tomatoes, chopped

½ small fennel bulb, sliced

1 potato, coarsely chopped

1 cup vegetable stock or water

4 cups chopped spinach or chard leaves

2 cans (19 oz/540 mL each) kidney beans, white beans, or chickpeas, rinsed and drained

In large saucepan, heat oil over medium-high heat. Add carrots and onion; cover and cook for 5 minutes. Stir in garlic, tarragon, mustard, thyme, and cayenne. Reduce heat to medium; cover and cook for 5 minutes more.

Stir in peppers, mushrooms, tomatoes, fennel, potato, and stock. Cover and cook until vegetables are tender-crisp, about 12 to 14 minutes. Stir in spinach and beans; cover and cook 3 minutes or until heated through.

Serve with rice or crusty bread.

Makes about 4 servings.

Veggie Noodles with Tomato Sauce

Marion Kane devised this clever meatless creation after tasting it in a restaurant. The vegetables are cut to resemble fettuccine noodles—hence the name. You can use all zucchini if you like; just increase to 2½ lb (1.25 kg). This is a vegan dish if you omit the butter. You can crumble goat cheese or sprinkle grated Parmesan over it before serving, if desired.

Sauce

1 can (28 oz/796 mL) tomatoes

1 tbsp butter

Salt and freshly ground black
    pepper to taste

Noodles

2 sweet red peppers

2 lb (1 kg) zucchini (about 6)

2 tbsp vegetable oil

2 tbsp dry sherry

1 tbsp rice vinegar

Salt and freshly ground
    black pepper to taste

For sauce, drain can of tomatoes, discarding juices. Place in food processor or blender and process until slightly chunky. Transfer to saucepan. Bring to a boil. Reduce heat to low and simmer for 10 minutes or until slightly thickened. Stir in butter. Add salt and pepper.

For noodles, using vegetable peeler cut peppers and zucchini lengthwise into thin slices, then cut slices into strips the width of fettuccine noodles, keeping peppers and zucchini separate.

In wok, heat oil over medium-high heat. Add pepper strips; stir-fry for 1 minute. Add zucchini; cook for 2 minutes, stirring gently. Pour in sherry and vinegar. Cover and cook for 2 to 3 minutes or until wilted but still crisp. Add salt and pepper.

Divide among 4 pasta bowls. Top with tomato sauce.

Makes 4 servings.

Stuffed Portobellos with Mushroom Gravy

This recipe comes from Allison Savage, whom we met when she organized a screening of the important documentary film Fresh, *featuring Michael Pollan, Will Allen, and Joel Salatin in an exploration of their practical visions of sustainable food production. Allison says she "believes strongly in the importance of food: good food, fresh food, real food." Her young daughter is her inspiration in wanting to help build a new food system.*

Serve this as a vegetarian main with salad and crusty bread or as a dinner party appetizer. Choose portobellos with cupped caps; it is harder to stuff flat caps.

1 sweet red pepper, cored and cut in large pieces

3 shallots, cut in half

1 zucchini, cut in 1-inch (2.5 cm) pieces

6 brown mushrooms, cut in half

2 tbsp olive oil

¼ tsp each: salt and freshly ground black pepper

2 cups fresh whole-grain breadcrumbs

1 cup grated Parmesan cheese

1 tbsp chopped fresh rosemary

1 tbsp chopped fresh thyme

3 cloves garlic, finely chopped

Salt and freshly ground black pepper to taste

6 large portobello mushrooms

Mushroom Gravy

2 tbsp olive oil

8 oz (250 g) assorted mushrooms (e.g., shiitake caps, oyster, brown), finely chopped

1 shallot, finely chopped

1 clove garlic, finely chopped

2 tbsp all-purpose flour

2½ cups vegetable stock

2 tbsp sherry (optional)

Salt and freshly ground black pepper to taste

Preheat oven to 425°F (220°C).

Place red pepper, shallots, zucchini, and brown mushrooms on large rimmed baking sheet. Drizzle with oil; sprinkle with ¼ teaspoon each salt and pepper. Roast in centre of oven for 20 to 25 minutes or until tender and golden. Cool. Finely chop. Leave oven on.

In large bowl, combine chopped roasted vegetable mixture, breadcrumbs, Parmesan, rosemary, thyme, garlic, and 3 tablespoons water. Add salt and pepper.

Remove and discard portobello stems. Using tip of spoon, scrape out and discard gills from undersides of portobello caps. Arrange caps in 13- × 9-inch (3 L) baking dish, stem side up. Stuff caps with roasted vegetable mixture, pressing mixture down firmly in each cap. Pour ¼ inch (5 mm) water into dish. Cover with foil. Bake in oven for 30 minutes or until mushrooms are tender.

Meanwhile, for gravy heat oil in frying pan over medium-high heat. Add mushrooms, shallot, and garlic; cook for 8 minutes or until vegetables are soft and all the liquid has been absorbed. Sprinkle with flour; continue to cook, stirring, for 1 to 2 minutes. Gradually whisk in stock. Cook, whisking, until mixture comes to a simmer. Cook for 2 to 3 minutes or until thickened. Stir in sherry (if using); cook 1 minute more. Add salt and pepper.

Turn oven to broil. Uncover mushrooms. Broil until tops are lightly browned, about 4 minutes, being careful not to burn. Remove from oven.

Serve stuffed mushrooms with mushroom gravy.

Makes 6 servings.

Roasted Celery Root Mash with Sautéed Mushrooms, Kale, and Pepper Purée

This elegant vegan entrée will impress your guests by showcasing a bounty of beautiful vegetables. It is shared by chef Jared Davis, who operated a terrific storefront vegan restaurant, Calico Café, right around the corner from FoodShare. Our staff were delighted to use the restaurant as an extension of the office, crossing the street to sit and have a meeting on Jared's patio, watch his garden grow, and eat his delectable food. The recipe that follows is worth all the steps involved in making it.

For more protein, add cooked beans to the mushroom mixture and garnish with toasted sliced almonds. It's as good as any meat dish and you can feel virtuous knowing that it costs you and the planet very little to make.

Mash

2 large celery roots, peeled and cut in cubes

1 cup chopped onion

½ cup diced celery

½ cup diced carrots

2 cloves garlic, finely chopped

3 sprigs fresh thyme

2 tbsp olive oil

1 cup vegetable stock

½ tsp each: salt and freshly ground black pepper

Yellow Pepper Purée

2 sweet yellow peppers, seeded and diced

2 tsp olive oil

½ cup chopped onion

¼ cup diced carrots

¼ cup diced celery

1 clove garlic, finely chopped

1 cup vegetable stock

Salt and freshly ground black pepper to taste

½ tsp fresh lemon juice

Red Pepper Purée

2 sweet red peppers, seeded and diced

2 tsp olive oil

½ cup chopped onion

¼ cup diced carrots

¼ cup diced celery

1 clove garlic, finely chopped

1 cup vegetable stock

Salt and freshly ground black pepper to taste

½ tsp fresh lemon juice

continued on next page

Mushrooms

3 tbsp olive oil

2 cloves garlic, finely chopped

4 cups (about 10 oz/300 g) sliced
    brown mushrooms or
    assorted mushrooms

Kale

½ cup vegetable stock

2 bunches Russian red kale or
    green curly kale, stemmed
    and chopped

2 cloves garlic, finely chopped

Salt and freshly ground black
    pepper to taste

Fresh sunflower sprouts (optional)

Preheat oven to 400°F (200°C).

For the mash, in large roasting pan combine celery roots with onion, celery, carrots, garlic, thyme, oil, half the stock, salt, and pepper. Cover with foil and bake for 20 minutes. Remove cover and continue to bake for 10 more minutes. Add remaining stock and mash with potato masher, or transfer to blender or food processor and pulse until smooth. Season with additional salt and pepper.

For the yellow pepper purée, in small frying pan on medium heat sauté peppers with oil, onion, carrots, celery, and garlic for 2 minutes. Deglaze with stock. Bring to a boil. Cover and simmer until all vegetables are soft, about 15 minutes. Purée in blender or food processor; season with salt and pepper to taste. Stir in lemon juice.

Repeat using red peppers for red pepper purée.

For the mushrooms, in large frying pan, heat oil to medium and sauté garlic for 1 minute. Add mushrooms and sauté until browned, about 5 minutes. Set aside.

For the kale, heat large saucepan or deep frying pan to medium; add stock, kale, and garlic. Cover and steam until wilted, about 2 to 3 minutes. Continue to cook uncovered until liquid is reduced. Season with salt and pepper.

To assemble, ladle each of the pepper sauces on a plate, place a large spoonful of mash in the centre, lean some kale against the mash and top with a spoonful of mushrooms. Garnish with sprouts (if using).

Makes 4 servings.

Butternut Squash and Chana Dal Curry

From Anuja Mendiratta, who worked at FoodShare in the 1990s and is now living in San Francisco. Anuja provided the research for executive director Debbie Field's Food 2002 Policy Recommendations: 28 policy recommendations and 28 grassroots program solutions to answer the question "What would it take for everyone in Ontario to have adequate access to healthy food?"

Anuja calls this exceptionally tasty dish "Manju's Butternut Squash and Chana Dal Curry," and sends it along with a story about her mother's way of cooking: "My mother, Manju Mendiratta, immigrated to the US from India in her 20s. In her new home on this continent, she became a wonderful self-taught cook of Punjabi and other Indian cuisines. My mother largely cooks by memory, hand, and taste, without written recipes or specific measurements. Over the years, I have watched and assisted her as she has cooked, absorbing as much as I can about her techniques, recipes, and ingredients. I have mastered only a few of her large repertoire of yummy dishes. This butternut squash curry is a particular favourite in that it is both savoury and sweet and benefits from protein through the dal. I have added my own flare and a bit of colour to the dish with the addition of fresh spinach."

½ cup chana dal (dried split chickpeas) or yellow split peas

¼ cup vegetable oil

1 large onion, diced

1 green chili, seeded and chopped

2 tsp ground cumin

2 tsp ground coriander

½ tsp turmeric

½ tsp salt

½ tsp freshly ground black pepper

1 cup chopped tomatoes

2 cloves garlic, finely chopped

1 tsp finely chopped ginger root

1 butternut squash, peeled, seeded, chopped in 1½-inch (4 cm) pieces

4 cups baby spinach

½ cup chopped fresh coriander

Place chana dal in bowl. Cover with water and soak for
30 minutes. Drain, rinse, and set aside.

In large frying pan, heat oil to medium. Add onion and sauté
until transparent, about 5 minutes. Add chili, cumin, coriander,
turmeric, salt, and pepper. Continue to cook for 3 minutes to
release flavours. Stir in tomatoes, garlic, and ginger; simmer to
form a thickened sauce.

Add squash and soaked chana dal. Simmer,
covered, for about 25 minutes or until squash and
chana dal are tender. If the mixture seems dry
add ½ cup water to the pan. The curry should be
thick but not dry.

Add spinach, cover with lid to steam for
2 minutes. Add coriander and stir to combine.

Serve with naan bread, raita (see page 86), and
chutney, if desired.

Lentil and Vegetable Curry Cup

This recipe was created by FoodShare chef Jesús Gomez with the assistance of Focus on Food youth intern Matthew Flannigan. Matthew represented FoodShare in the inaugural Toronto Youth Food Policy Council competition So You(th) Think You Can Cook, at the Royal Agricultural Winter Fair, and won first place. Here is the award-winning recipe, which features a delicate squash that can be eaten skin and all.

4 delicata or acorn squash, cut in half lengthwise, seeds removed, bottoms trimmed to sit flat

¼ cup olive oil

½ onion, diced

3 cloves garlic, finely chopped

1 carrot, diced

1½ cups peeled and diced potatoes

1 tsp curry powder

¼ tsp each: chili powder, ground cumin, and paprika

1½ cups cooked green lentils or 1 can (19 oz/540mL), rinsed and drained

½ sweet red pepper, diced

Salt and freshly ground black pepper to taste

1½ cups coconut milk or 1 can (14 oz/398 mL)

½ cup vegetable stock

¼ cup chopped fresh parsley

Preheat oven to 350°F (180°C).

Brush each squash half with ½ teaspoon of oil and place on baking sheet lined with parchment paper or foil. Bake until flesh is tender and can be pierced with a fork, about 30 minutes

Meanwhile, heat remaining oil on medium heat and sauté onion and garlic until transparent, about 5 minutes. Add carrot, potatoes, curry powder, chili powder, cumin, and paprika. Cook 5 minutes more; add lentils, red pepper, and a good pinch of salt and pepper. Cook 2 minutes more.

Stir in coconut milk and vegetable stock. Simmer for another 5 minutes or until carrot and potatoes are tender and sauce has thickened. Season with salt and pepper.

Divide lentil mixture among squash halves to fill. Sprinkle with parsley and serve.

Makes 8 servings.

Pumpkin Leaves in Peanut Butter Sauce with Millet Sadza

Tinashe Kanengoni was the first community food security co-ordinator to work for the City of Toronto in the Toronto Community Food Animation program, under which he helped to organize food security initiatives for 5 years in the Lawrence Heights community. The Afri-Can Food Basket and the Stop Community Food Centre have been key partners with FoodShare in the program, helping to start community gardens, markets, and kitchens in low-income neighbourhoods.

Tinashe has also done food security work in Zimbabwe, Botswana, Zambia, and Kenya, and shared this traditional childhood recipe from Zimbabwe, where he is now working.

1 cup millet, rinsed and drained

1½ tsp salt

1 lb (about 500 g) young, soft pumpkin leaves or collard greens

1 onion, finely chopped

½ tsp curry powder (optional)

2 tomatoes, each cut into 8 wedges

½ tsp salt

⅓ cup creamy peanut butter

For the sadza, add 6 cups of water to medium saucepan and bring to a boil. Add millet and salt. Reduce heat and simmer uncovered for 45 to 50 minutes, stirring occasionally, until a thick, porridge-like consistency is achieved. Keep warm until ready to serve.

Wash pumpkin leaves thoroughly in cold water and let them drip try. Remove threads by breaking off stems and pulling strings down the leaf. Thinly slice leaves.

In large frying pan, bring 1 cup water to a boil. Add leaves and onion; reduce heat to low, cover and steam for 10 minutes. Add curry powder (if using), tomatoes, and remaining ½ teaspoon salt; cover and continue to steam for 5 minutes.

Add peanut butter and stir until well combined. Simmer uncovered for another 5 to 10 minutes or until the mixture has thickened. Serve over a scoop of reserved hot sadza.

Makes 4 servings.

Egyptian Koshary

Koshary, a delectable vegan meal of rice, lentils, and pasta layered in a spicy tomato sauce, is arguably Egypt's national dish due to its popularity and availability, but it is almost unknown outside the country. Mary Roufail, community food animator co-ordinator at FoodShare, considers it the perfect food. She passed along this recipe after a recent trip to Egypt to visit relatives. It's most commonly eaten as a hearty, inexpensive fast meal and is widely available in the local eateries that line the streets.

Mary and her colleagues in FoodShare's Community Food Animation program help to organize community gardens, mid-scale composting, and community kitchens and markets in low-income neighbourhoods, and they facilitate training and networking.

5 tbsp vegetable oil

¾ cup long-grain white rice

3 tsp salt

¾ cup elbow macaroni

3 onions, thinly sliced

3 cloves garlic, finely chopped

6 large tomatoes, finely chopped, or 1 can (28 oz/796 mL) crushed tomatoes

¼ cup tomato paste

¼ cup white vinegar

1 tsp freshly ground black pepper

4 tsp ground cumin

¼ tsp cayenne pepper

2 cups cooked brown lentils, warm, or 1 can (19 oz/540mL), rinsed, drained, heated

In small saucepan, heat 2 teaspoons oil over medium heat. Add rice; stir until coated with oil and lightly toasted, about 3 minutes. Add 1½ cups water and ½ teaspoon salt and bring to a boil. Reduce heat, cover, and simmer for 20 to 25 minutes until the rice is tender. Fluff with a fork and set aside.

In medium saucepan, bring to a boil 4 cups of water and add 1 teaspoon salt. Add macaroni; cook approximately 8 minutes or until tender. Drain, return to pot, cover to keep warm.

In large frying pan on medium-high, heat 3 tablespoons oil. Sauté onions until caramelized and crisp, 15 to 20 minutes. Remove onions from pan, drain on a paper towel–lined plate, and set aside.

To the same pan, add remaining oil and garlic. Sauté on medium heat for 1 minute. Add tomatoes, tomato paste, vinegar, remaining salt, pepper, cumin, and cayenne. Bring to a boil. Reduce heat and simmer for 10 minutes.

To serve, assemble koshary in a large bowl or platter, layering the ingredients starting with rice, then macaroni, lentils, and tomato sauce; top with reserved fried onions.

Makes 6 servings.

Pasta e Fagioli

Food stylist and recipe tester Lesleigh Landry offers her version of a traditional Italian pasta and bean dish, which is a staple at her house. She likes to use two different kinds of beans (white kidney beans mash well), and serves it with a non-traditional chipotle hot sauce on the side. Leftovers absorb liquid, so thin with additional stock when reheating.

2 cans (19 oz/540 mL each) beans
    (e.g., white kidney, red kidney,
    Romano), rinsed and drained

2 tbsp olive oil

3 slices bacon, chopped

1 cup chopped carrots

1 cup chopped celery

1 onion, chopped

3 cloves garlic, finely chopped

6 cups chicken stock

1½ cups pasta shells, tubetti, or
    other small pasta

Salt and freshly ground black
    pepper to taste

Grated Parmesan cheese (optional)

Mash half the beans with potato masher. Set aside.

In large saucepan, heat oil over medium-high heat. Cook bacon, carrots, celery, onion, and garlic for 7 to 10 minutes or until lightly browned, stirring frequently. Stir in stock along with mashed and whole beans. Bring to a boil. Stir in pasta; cook for 8 minutes or until pasta is tender but firm.

Remove from heat. Add salt and pepper. Serve sprinkled with Parmesan (if using).

Make about 6 servings.

Pasta with Beans and Greens

This easy-to-make entrée is packed with healthful ingredients. It's just the kind of versatile and nutrient-rich dish that Adrienne likes to compose, taking her lead from whatever ingredients she picks fresh from the garden, gathers at a farmers' market, or has on hand, often turning to beans as an important source of protein. Some can find the idea of vegan cooking intimidating or off-putting for a variety of reasons, but this dish is a testament to the ease of making vegan meals—and the joy of eating them. Try it with a variety of greens or a shake here and there of celery seed, Hungarian paprika, chili flakes, or Japanese seven-spice (shichimi togarashi), or some torn basil leaves. You will need a very large frying pan.

2 cups short pasta (e.g., fusilli, rotini, penne, farfalle)

2 tbsp olive oil

3 cloves garlic, finely chopped

1 bunch green onions, chopped

1 can (19 oz/540 mL) chopped tomatoes

1 bunch fresh spinach or 1 package (10 oz/300 g) frozen, chopped

1 can (19 oz/540 mL) Romano, cannellini, or other beans, rinsed and drained

1 tbsp balsamic vinegar

½ tsp salt

¼ tsp freshly ground black pepper

In large saucepan of boiling salted water, cook pasta about 8 minutes or until tender but firm. Drain.

Meanwhile, heat oil in large frying pan over medium heat. Cook garlic and green onions for 2 minutes or until softened, stirring occasionally. Add tomatoes and their juice. Cook for 5 minutes. Stir in spinach; cook 2 to 3 minutes or until wilted. Add drained pasta, beans, vinegar, salt, and pepper. Cook about 5 minutes or until heated through.

Makes 6 servings.

Dan Dan Noodles

This version of dan dan noodles is a one-bowl dish for spice lovers that you can make in less than 30 minutes. It's a favourite recipe from Felicia Quon inspired by Fuchsia Dunlop's book Shark's Fin and Sichuan Pepper: A Sweet-Sour Memoir of Eating in China *and other sources. Says Quon, "Noodles are my comfort food. I'll never tire of them." Buy refrigerated noodles, not the dried kind. Thicker-cut Shanghai noodles are ideal, but you could also use udon. Many Chinese groceries sell fresh noodles; package sizes vary. Tahini (sesame seed paste) is sold in most supermarkets and Middle Eastern food shops. Some recipes chill the noodles before serving with the hot meat topping.*

6 cups sliced baby bok choy

10 oz (300 g) fresh Asian wheat noodles

1 tbsp vegetable oil

8 oz (250 g) lean ground pork

1 tbsp finely chopped ginger root

½ cup chicken stock

2 tbsp tahini

1 tbsp soy sauce

2 tsp Asian chili sauce, or to taste

½ cup chopped fresh coriander

2 green onions, thinly sliced

Place bok choy in colander; set in sink.

In large saucepan of boiling water, cook noodles until tender but firm. (Time will depend on type and thickness of noodles.)

Meanwhile, in frying pan, heat oil over medium-high heat. Cook pork for 2 minutes, stirring to break it up. Stir in ginger; cook for 2 minutes more. Stir in stock, tahini, soy sauce, and chili sauce. Reduce heat to low; simmer for 5 minutes or until sauce thickens.

Pour cooked noodles and their cooking water over bok choy in colander to wilt. Transfer noodles and bok choy to serving platter. Pour meat mixture on top. Sprinkle with coriander and green onions.

Makes about 4 servings.

Ricotta Gnocchi

This fantastic dish comes from Mary Lou Morgan and her mother-in-law, Armida Morgan. Mary Lou worked at FoodShare from 1992 to 2005 and developed many of our programs, including the Good Food Box, Field to Table Catering, and the Focus on Food youth program. She always made this dish with our youth interns, in the best Italian tradition, taking plenty of time to enjoy the experience of talking and working together—and of course to savour the tasty results. Serve with a pasta sauce of your choice and grated Parmesan. Shaping the gnocchi takes a bit of practice, but the ridges are traditional and help the gnocchi hold the sauce.

1 lb (500 g) ricotta cheese

1 egg

2 cups all-purpose flour

Pinch nutmeg

Pinch salt

Tomato sauce or butter for serving

In bowl, stir together ricotta and egg. Add flour, nutmeg, and salt. Using your hands, mix gently until dough begins to hold together. Divide dough into 6 equal pieces.

On floured work surface, roll one piece of dough into rope about the thickness of your thumb. Cut crosswise into little pillow-shaped pieces about ¾ inch (2 cm) long. Place a dinner fork tines down on floured work surface. One at a time, roll each gnocchi down the back of the fork tines to make indentations. If gnocchi are too sticky to shape, roll each piece in a bit of flour. Place shaped pieces well apart on large rimmed baking sheet between layers of waxed paper. Repeat with remaining dough pieces.

Place in freezer for at least 15 minutes. (Once they are frozen solid, you can place in freezer bags to cook another day.)

In large saucepan of boiling salted water, cook one-quarter of gnocchi for 5 to 6 minutes or until they rise to the surface. Using slotted spoon, transfer to serving bowl with a little tomato sauce or butter to prevent them from sticking together. Place in warm oven as you cook each batch. Add more sauce just before serving.

Makes about 6 servings.

Squash Risotto

A sweet, simple, and toothsome recipe contributed by a group of employees from a corporate organization who visited FoodShare to help one day and decided that they wanted to do even more. As a proud United Way Toronto agency, FoodShare has the opportunity to work with some fantastic corporate volunteers, so it was no surprise when this wonderful group visited and helped us pack Good Food Boxes. We were delighted when they were so impressed with FoodShare's work that they put together their own cookbook to help with ours. This recipe comes from that collection. Substitute stock for the white wine if desired.

1 butternut squash, peeled, seeded, cut in cubes (about 6 cups)

2 tbsp olive oil

Salt and freshly ground black pepper to taste

8 cups chicken or vegetable stock

4 tbsp butter

1 small onion, finely diced

2 cups arborio rice

1 cup dry white wine

½ cup grated Parmesan cheese

1 tbsp butter

Preheat oven to 425°F (220°C).

In large bowl, toss squash with oil. Spread onto large rimmed baking sheet in single layer. Bake in oven for 30 minutes or until tender and lightly golden. Add salt and pepper. Set aside.

In large saucepan, heat stock over medium heat.

In another large saucepan, melt butter over medium heat. Add onion; cook for 4 to 6 minutes or until softened, stirring occasionally. Add rice; cook for 2 minutes, stirring. Add wine; cook for 3 minutes or until most of liquid is absorbed, stirring constantly. Add hot stock ½ cup at a time, stirring constantly after each addition until liquid is absorbed and adjusting heat under pan to maintain a simmer.

Continue adding stock, cooking and stirring until rice is tender and creamy but with a slight bite at the centre, about 18 minutes. (You may have stock left over.) Stir in squash, Parmesan, and remaining tablespoon of butter. Season with more salt and pepper.

Makes about 6 servings.

Poached Eggs with Bacon Rösti and Tomatoes

From a leader of the slow food and local food movements, dedicated and original Toronto chef Jamie Kennedy, comes this delicious potato pancake dish that's great for breakfast, lunch, or dinner. Use top-quality organic potatoes, tomatoes, and eggs for the best flavour. Jamie uses slab bacon and cuts it into lardons; it can be hard to find so we substituted thick-cut sliced bacon. The right size of non-stick frying pan is key for rösti. With each rösti the pan will get hotter so you may have to reduce heat to ensure that each one cooks through and crisps up without burning. A bit fiddly but worth the effort.

8 oz (250 g) thick-sliced bacon (about 5 slices)

2 shallots, diced

6 Yukon Gold potatoes, peeled

6 tbsp unsalted butter

6 tomatoes

Salt and freshly ground black pepper to taste

2 tbsp white vinegar

12 eggs, at room temperature

Preheat oven to 300°F (150°C).

Cut bacon strips crosswise into ¼-inch (5 mm) pieces. Place in cold frying pan. Turn heat to medium and cook, stirring occasionally, until pieces start to crisp, about 12 minutes. Stir in shallots; cook another 2 minutes. Using slotted spoon, transfer mixture to paper towel to drain, and set aside.

In 8-inch (20 cm) heavy-bottomed, non-stick frying pan, melt 1 tablespoon of butter over medium heat. Meanwhile, shred one potato onto a clean tea towel using large holes of box grater. Gather up tea towel and twist to squeeze out as much water as possible. Distribute potato in frying pan. Add one-sixth of bacon mixture, distributing evenly. Using spatula, press into even layer. Cook until brown at edges, about 5 to 6 minutes. Turn over carefully; cook another 5 to 6 minutes. Place on large rimmed baking sheet in oven to keep warm. Repeat with remaining butter, potatoes, and bacon mixture to make 6 rösti.

Thickly slice tomatoes and place on plate. Season with salt and pepper. Set aside.

In shallow, wide saucepan, bring 2 inches (5 cm) water to a boil. Add vinegar. Reduce heat to simmer. Gently break eggs into simmering water. Cook to desired doneness, between 4 and 7 minutes. Adjust temperature as necessary to maintain a simmer.

Place one rösti on each of six plates. Arrange tomato slices on top of each rösti in a circular pattern, dividing evenly among the plates. Top each with two poached eggs. Sprinkle with more salt and pepper.

Makes 6 servings.

Chicken Marbella with Prunes, Olives, and Capers

The FoodShare kitchen makes a version of this in large batches, led by chef Jesús Gomez. A profoundly philosophical leader who is often found surrounded by youth interns as part of our Focus on Food program, Jesús speaks volumes through the art of his food. Youth follow his directions with awe and pleasure as he patiently conveys how to lovingly prepare this dish, in which prunes, olives, and capers add the perfect zingy complement to chicken. It's a stellar party dish or potluck offering. Use 4 small or 3 medium chickens. Use cured olives, not canned, and either black or green will do just fine.

4 chickens (2½ lb/1.25 kg each), each cut in 8 pieces

1 cup pitted prunes

1 cup pitted cured olives

½ cup drained capers, juices reserved

6 bay leaves

1 head garlic, finely chopped

¼ cup dried oregano

1 tsp kosher salt

½ tsp freshly ground black pepper

½ cup red wine vinegar

½ cup olive oil

1 cup brown sugar

1 cup dry white wine

¼ cup chopped fresh flat-leaf parsley or coriander

In large bowl, combine chicken, prunes, olives, capers and a dash of the caper juice, bay leaves, garlic, oregano, salt, pepper, vinegar, and oil. Stir well to coat chicken. Cover and chill overnight.

Preheat oven to 350°F (180°C).

Arrange chicken in a single layer in 2 or 3 roasting pans or baking dishes. Spoon prune/olive mixture over it evenly. Sprinkle with brown sugar and pour wine around chicken.

Bake for 50 minutes to 1 hour, basting several times with pan juices, and switching pans top to bottom halfway through cooking time. Remove bay leaves.

Sprinkle with parsley or coriander and serve with pasta or mashed potatoes.

Makes 10 to 12 servings.

Jerk Chicken

A favourite recipe from chef Sybil Pinnock, a member of FoodShare's kitchen team. This rendition of a Caribbean staple has a rich, tangy sauce. The love and joy that Sybil brings to everything she does is evident here, in a spicy dish that has become a signature of FoodShare's Field to Table Catering. It's also a favourite with the Grade 7 and 8 students in FoodShare's cafeteria program, the Good Food Café.

2 tbsp garlic powder

1 tbsp granulated sugar

1 tbsp ground allspice

1 tbsp dried thyme

1½ tsp hot pepper flakes

1½ tsp freshly ground
    black pepper

1 tsp salt

¾ tsp cinnamon

½ cup orange juice

⅓ cup apple cider vinegar

¼ cup olive oil

¼ cup soy sauce

Juice of 1 lemon or lime
    (about 3–4 tbsp)

1 onion, finely chopped

3 green onions, finely chopped

1 Scotch bonnet pepper,
    seeded and finely chopped

2 chickens, each cut in
    8 serving pieces

In 13- × 9-inch (3 L) baking dish, whisk together garlic powder, sugar, allspice, thyme, hot pepper flakes, pepper, salt, cinnamon, orange juice, vinegar, oil, soy sauce, lemon juice, onion, green onions, and Scotch bonnet pepper. Place chicken pieces in marinade, turning to coat. Cover with plastic wrap. Chill for at least 4 hours or up to 24 hours.

Preheat barbecue to medium heat. Remove chicken from marinade and place on oiled grill, reserving marinade. Close barbecue lid; cook for 25 minutes or until cooked through, turning pieces occasionally.

Meanwhile, place reserved marinade in saucepan. Bring to a boil. Reduce heat to simmer and cook for 5 minutes. Pour over cooked chicken or serve as sauce on the side.

Serve with mashed potatoes, rice and peas, or noodles.

Makes about 8 servings.

Chicken Adobo

A Filipino staple adapted from a recipe by Jocelyn Cerezo of the Alexandra Park community, where cooking and growing together have built a strong neighbourhood. This has feisty flavour and tastes even better made a day or two ahead.

3 lb (1.5 kg) chicken, cut in 8 pieces

⅔ cup apple cider vinegar

⅓ cup soy sauce

¼ cup orange juice

5 bay leaves

¼ cup vegetable oil

1 head garlic, cloves separated and chopped

1 small onion, diced

Few slices peeled ginger root

1 cup diced sweet red pepper

2 tbsp cornstarch

In large bowl, combine chicken, vinegar, soy sauce, orange juice, and bay leaves, turning chicken to coat. Cover and marinate in fridge for 1 hour or overnight.

In wok or large saucepan, heat half the oil over medium heat. Add garlic, onion, and ginger; cook for 4 minutes or until softened. Add chicken with marinade and red pepper. Bring to a boil. Reduce heat to medium-low, cover, and simmer for 20 minutes or until chicken is cooked through. Using tongs, remove chicken from sauce. Keep sauce warm over medium-low heat.

Meanwhile, in large frying pan, heat remaining oil over medium-high heat. Cook chicken for 4 minutes or until well browned, turning once. Return browned chicken to sauce in wok.

In small bowl, dissolve cornstarch in 3 tablespoons cold water. Stir into chicken mixture. Bring to a boil. Reduce heat to low and cook uncovered for 5 minutes. Remove and discard bay leaves.

Serve hot with plain rice.

Makes 4 to 6 servings.

Persian Chicken and Walnut Stew (Khoresh)

In this classic dish from Iran, passed along by FoodShare's director of social enterprise Zahra Parvinian, walnuts, pomegranate, and saffron provide a refreshing counterpoint to chicken. Look for pomegranate paste in Middle Eastern grocery stores.

2 cups walnut halves

4 tsp butter or vegetable oil

2 lb (1 kg) boneless skinless chicken thighs, cut in half

2 large onions, thinly sliced

1 tsp salt

½ tsp turmeric

½ tsp cinnamon

½ cup pomegranate paste, pomegranate molasses, or pomegranate syrup

¼ tsp saffron threads

2 tsp granulated sugar (optional)

In food processor, finely grind walnuts. Set aside.

Heat butter over medium heat in a Dutch oven or casserole dish; add chicken and onions and brown, turning once, about 4 to 5 minutes. Add salt, turmeric, and cinnamon. Reduce heat to low, add ground walnuts, and stir to combine. Add pomegranate paste, saffron, and 1½ cups water.

Simmer, covered, for 30 minutes or until sauce has thickened and chicken is very tender. Taste the sauce and adjust for seasoning, adding sugar if too sour.

Serve over cooked rice.

Makes 4 servings.

The Ultimate Roast Turkey

Marion Kane developed this recipe, which she has honed and simplified over time. Fresh rather than frozen turkey is best, as naturally raised as possible. Cheesecloth is sold in most cookware stores and supermarkets. While the turkey is roasting, make stock by simmering neck and innards (except liver) along with a carrot, a small onion, and herbs of your choice in water to cover for at least 2 hours. Strain and discard solids. For gravy, red currant or black currant jam is best but others, such as raspberry, would be fine. The wine in this special dish makes it a splurge.

1 cup butter

1 bottle (750 mL) dry white wine

About 20 lb (9 kg) turkey

Kosher salt

Gravy

3 tbsp all-purpose flour

3 cups homemade turkey stock

1 tbsp jam or jelly

Kosher salt and freshly ground black pepper to taste

Preheat oven to 325°F (160°C).

Cut piece of cheesecloth to form 4 layers about 18 inches (46 cm) square.

In saucepan, melt butter with wine over medium-low heat. Place cheesecloth in saucepan; let soak.

Place turkey breast side up on wire rack in roasting pan. Sprinkle with salt. Place soaked cheesecloth on top to cover breast and legs.

Roast in oven 4 to 4½ hours, basting every 30 minutes with butter/wine mixture until juices run clear or thermometer placed in thickest part of thigh (do not touch bone) registers 180°F (82°C) for stuffed turkey, 170°F (77°C) for unstuffed.

Remove turkey from oven. Carefully peel off cheesecloth. Let stand about 15 minutes.

Transfer cooked turkey on its wire rack to cutting board.

For gravy, drain and discard all but about ¼ cup of drippings from roasting pan. Place pan on stove over medium-low heat. Add flour; whisk until smooth. Add stock. Bring to a boil. Reduce heat to medium-low, whisking and scraping up browned bits from pan until smooth and thickened. Add jam, salt, and pepper; stir to combine. Pour gravy through sieve; discard solids. Makes about 3 cups.

Carve turkey and serve with gravy.

Makes 12 to 14 servings.

Oven-Roasted Fish

An excellent, Portuguese-inspired creation from Linda Haynes, prolific cookbook author and founder, with partner Martin Connell, of ACE Bakery, whose foundation has been a key supporter of FoodShare's community cooking programs over the years. With their help, FoodShare has been able to work deeply in communities to build capacity and teach thousands to feed themselves.

3 large Yukon Gold potatoes, peeled and thinly sliced

2 cans (28 oz/796 mL each) whole tomatoes

2 tbsp olive oil

1 large onion, thinly sliced

2 cloves garlic, grated

6 whole basil leaves

½ cup dry white wine

⅛ tsp freshly ground black pepper

1 tbsp olive oil

2½ lb (1.25 kg) cod fillet, cut into 8 portions

¼ tsp salt

¼ tsp freshly ground black pepper

½ cup chopped fresh basil

⅓ cup chopped fresh parsley

2 tsp finely grated lemon rind

Preheat oven to 375°F (190°C).

Bring saucepan of salted water to a boil. Add potatoes; cook for 5 to 7 minutes or until just barely cooked through. Drain.

Drain tomatoes, reserving juice, and slice.

In very large frying pan, heat 2 tablespoons of oil over medium heat. Add onion; cook for 4 to 5 minutes or until softened but not coloured. Stir in garlic; cook for 30 seconds. Stir in tomatoes with reserved juice, basil, wine, and ⅛ teaspoon pepper. Bring to a boil. Reduce heat to low and simmer uncovered for 20 minutes, stirring occasionally.

In 13- × 9-inch (3 L) baking dish, arrange potato slices, overlapping them.

In another large frying pan, heat remaining tablespoon of oil over medium-high heat. Sprinkle cod with salt and ¼ teaspoon pepper. In batches, sear fish until golden, about 1 minute per side. Place fish on top of potatoes in baking dish. Spoon tomato sauce over fish.

Bake in centre of oven for 15 to 20 minutes or until fish is cooked through. Remove from oven. Sprinkle with basil, parsley, and lemon rind.

Serve with thick slices of crusty bread to soak up juices.

Make about 8 servings.

Lahori Fish

Ayesha Khalid, one of FoodShare's student nutrition animators, passed along this traditional dish from Lahore, Pakistan. Ayesha came to FoodShare after organizing a mid-morning meal program at George B. Little Public School in Scarborough, where her two children go to school. As a student nutrition animator, she now helps other parents and schools organize sustainable school nutrition programs, passing on the many skills she and our other animators have developed over the years so programs don't have to reinvent the wheel.

In Pakistan, this dish can be found everywhere from big restaurants to vendors outside the old historical bazaars and at outdoor markets. It can be traced back to the Mughal regime, which influenced the cuisine in Lahore. Lahori fish is usually fried and very crispy, but in this recipe it is baked because Ayesha's mom is very health conscious and has modified the preparation.

2 cloves garlic, finely chopped

2 lb (1 kg) white fish, cut in 2-inch (5 cm) chunks

1 cup besan (chickpea flour)

2 tsp red chili flakes (optional)

1 tsp ground cumin

1 tsp ground coriander

1 tsp garam masala

2 tsp salt

1 tsp turmeric

2 tbsp rice flour

Vegetable oil for frying

In large bowl, combine garlic with ¼ cup water. Add fish, cover with plastic wrap, and marinate for 10 minutes at room temperature.

In medium bowl, mix besan, chili flakes, cumin, coriander, garam masala, salt, turmeric, and rice flour.

Dip fish pieces into besan mixture to coat. Transfer to large plate, cover with plastic wrap, and refrigerate for 30 minutes.

Preheat oven to 350°F (180°C).

Place fish on lightly greased or parchment-lined large rimmed baking sheet. Bake for 8 to 10 minutes, turning once, until golden brown.

Serve with a sweet and sour dipping sauce, such as tamarind sauce (see page 77).

Makes 4 to 6 servings.

West Coast Teriyaki Salmon with Wasabi Mayonnaise

From Laura Kalina in Kamloops, British Columbia, comes this easy and healthy way of preparing salmon. Wasabi powder can be found in the Asian aisle of the grocery store.

Like many dieticians across Canada, Laura is the backbone of local food security organizing in her community. Through involvement in Kamloops FoodShare (a program associated with the Kamloops food bank), she develops community-based programs such as community kitchens and gardens. Through the Kamloops Food Policy Council, she leads municipal policy initiatives like getting Kamloops City Council to adopt a food charter, the second municipality to do so after Toronto.

½ cup orange juice

3 tbsp low-sodium soy sauce

2 tbsp brown sugar or maple syrup

2 cloves garlic, finely chopped

2 tsp grated ginger root

4 salmon fillets (each 4–5 oz/150 g), skinned and deboned

½ tsp wasabi powder

¼ cup mayonnaise

For teriyaki marinade, in small bowl stir together orange juice, soy sauce, brown sugar, garlic, and ginger.

Place salmon in shallow dish; pour marinade over top. Set aside for 30 minutes, turning the salmon twice in the marinade.

In another small bowl, combine wasabi powder with 1 teaspoon water to create a paste. Add mayonnaise; stir to combine. Place in the fridge.

Preheat oven to 425°F (220°C).

Remove salmon from marinade and place on lightly greased or parchment-lined rimmed baking sheet. Bake until fish is just opaque and cooked through, about 10 minutes per inch (2.5 cm) of thickness.

Serve with wasabi mayonnaise on the side.

Makes 4 servings.

Bouillabaisse

Contributed by the late Jack Layton, a lover of food and one of the first Canadian political and social leaders to understand the importance of the food movement. He championed many important food policies, helping to found the Toronto Food Policy Council and with his partner, Olivia Chow, particularly supported FoodShare's work organizing student nutrition programs. When he submitted the recipe, Jack's note suggested cooking with sustainable fish. You can buy seafood stock at many fish stores; if using bouillon cubes, make the stock half strength.

1 large pinch saffron (optional)

2 tbsp orange juice (optional)

2 tbsp olive oil

2 cloves garlic, smashed

1 large onion, sliced

1 small fennel bulb, thinly sliced

1 strip orange rind

1¾ cups canned chopped tomatoes

4–6 small potatoes, peeled and cut in ½-inch (1 cm) cubes

6 cups seafood stock or clam juice

1 lb (500 g) halibut, cod, or snapper, cut in large chunks

8 large shrimp, peeled and deveined

8 clams or mussels

1 bunch flat-leaf parsley, chopped

If using, soak saffron in orange juice for 10 minutes.

In large heavy-bottomed saucepan, heat oil over medium-high heat. Cook garlic, onion, and fennel until golden, about 5 to 10 minutes. Stir in saffron mixture (if using), orange rind, tomatoes and their juice, potatoes, and stock. Bring to a boil. Reduce heat to medium and cook uncovered until vegetables are tender and liquid is reduced by half, about 20 minutes.

Stir in fish (but not shellfish). Cover and cook for 2 minutes. Stir in shellfish; cover and cook for 4 minutes or until shells open and fish is cooked through.

Sprinkle with parsley. Ladle into bowls. Serve with crusty bread.

Makes about 4 servings.

Chinese Fried Rice

This recipe comes from Toronto chef Winlai Wong, who has been a big supporter of FoodShare's work to bring Food Literacy to Ontario students, participating in our Recipe for Change fundraiser and joining us on the front lawn of Queen's Park for Eat-In Ontario, a day of curriculum-linked and tasting activities for students from JK to Grade 12. Winlai's father and mentor, Manfred Wong, showed Marion Kane how to make this perfect rendition of a Chinese staple. The ideal way to use up leftovers. You could use a small amount of chicken stock instead of the bouillon cube.

¼ **cup vegetable oil**

6 oz (175 g) **shiitake mushrooms, stems removed and coarsely chopped (about 2 cups)**

8 oz (250 g) **shrimp, peeled, deveined, coarsely chopped**

3 large **eggs, lightly beaten**

2 cups **fresh or frozen peas**

8 oz (250 g) **Chinese barbecued pork or ham, chopped**

6 cups **cooked rice, clumps broken up with fingers**

½ **cube chicken or vegetable bouillon, crumbled**

4 **green onions, chopped**

1 tbsp **light soy sauce**

1 tbsp **oyster sauce**

Heat wok over medium-high heat. When very hot, add 1 tablespoon of oil. Add mushrooms; cook, stirring and shaking, until golden brown, about 2 minutes. Transfer to bowl.

Add 2 tablespoons of oil to wok. Add shrimp; cook, stirring and shaking, just until opaque, about 1 minute. Add to mushrooms in bowl.

Add 1 teaspoon of oil to wok. Add beaten eggs; cook, without stirring, until they begin to set, about 20 seconds. Using fork or metal spatula, scramble eggs, then break into small pieces, cooking until cooked through but not browned, about 1 minute more. Transfer to small bowl.

Add remaining oil to wok. Add peas and barbecued pork; cook, stirring and shaking, about 30 seconds. Add rice and bouillon cube; cook, stirring, shaking, and breaking up clumps in rice, for about 3 minutes. Reduce heat to medium. Return mushrooms, shrimp, and eggs to wok; cook, stirring and shaking, for about 1 minute. Stir in green onions. Remove from heat.

In small bowl, stir together soy sauce and oyster sauce; stir into fried rice and serve.

Makes 4 to 6 servings.

*share * mains*

Louisiana Gumbo

Harriet Friedmann, sociology professor at the University of Toronto and an internationally recognized expert on the economy of food, shares this slightly complicated but authentic recipe, which she believes captures something of the cultural mix that happens in unique ways in Toronto and across Canada. Harriet tells us that the word gumbo is derived from an African word for okra, the most important ingredient in this dish and a plant that is now being grown in Ontario. This meal is a favourite because it reminds Harriet of her childhood in Baton Rouge and visits to a friend's Cajun grandmother who lived in the country where big nets full of squirming shrimp were hauled onto the pier.

You can use chorizo, kielbasa, or other smoked sausage in place of andouille. If you prefer more seafood, use 1 lb (500 g) crab or whitefish in place of chicken.

2 lb (1 kg) medium shrimp

1 tbsp butter

5 oz (150 g) okra, sliced in 1-inch (2.5 cm) rounds

1 tbsp white vinegar

½ cup butter

½ cup all-purpose flour

1 onion, chopped

1 bunch green onions, chopped

½ cup chopped celery

1 lb (500 g) andouille sausage, sliced in ¼-inch (5 mm) rounds

1 lb (500 g) boneless skinless chicken thighs, cut in bite-sized pieces

1 tbsp finely chopped fresh parsley

1 tsp freshly ground black pepper

½ tsp cayenne pepper

Salt to taste

Cooked white rice (about 4 cups)

Filé powder (optional)

Peel and devein shrimp, saving shells. Return shrimp to fridge. In large soup pot, boil shrimp shells in 10 cups water until reduced to about 3 cups of liquid, about 30 minutes. Strain liquid into another saucepan, discarding shells. Set aside.

In frying pan, melt 1 tablespoon butter over medium-high heat. Cook okra for 2 minutes or until starting to turn brown. Remove from heat and stir in vinegar. Set aside.

In large heavy-bottomed stock pot, melt ½ cup butter over medium heat. Stir in flour. Cook, stirring constantly for 5 minutes or until mixture is medium brown, about the colour of peanut butter. Stir in onion, green onions, and celery; cook, stirring occasionally, until browned, about 10 minutes. Add sausage; cook for 3 minutes. Stir in reduced shrimp liquid, chicken, parsley, pepper, and cayenne. Bring to a boil. Reduce heat to medium-low and cook uncovered for 30 minutes, stirring frequently so it doesn't stick to bottom of pan.

Stir shrimp into gumbo. Return to a boil. Reduce heat to simmer and cook 2 minutes or until shrimp are cooked through. Add salt.

Place ½ cup cooked rice in each bowl. Ladle gumbo on top. Sprinkle with pinch of filé powder (if using).

Makes 8 servings.

Indian-Spiced Shrimp

This lusciously light and refreshing dish is from Art Eggleton, who was instrumental in creating FoodShare in 1985 when he was mayor of Toronto. FoodShare is now working with Senator Eggleton and others across the country to build the case for a Canadian national student and child nutrition policy.

Art is a big fan of spicy food and this recipe is the creation of his wife, Camille Bacchus, who calls it "Art's Indian-Spiced Shrimp" because it is his favourite. Increase the jalapeño if you find it too mild. You could add a little coconut milk or whipping cream to the sauce before adding shrimp. Substitute canned diced tomatoes if you like. If this is a main course, serve over rice or noodles with a green salad.

1 tbsp olive oil

1 onion, chopped

1 tbsp seeded, chopped jalapeño

1 tsp finely chopped ginger root

1 clove garlic, finely chopped

1 tsp ground coriander

1 tsp ground cumin

1 tsp garam masala

⅛ tsp turmeric

1 lb (500 g) plum tomatoes,
    chopped (about 2¾ cups)

3 tbsp chicken or vegetable stock

2 tbsp fresh lemon juice

Salt to taste

1 lb (500 g) large shrimp, peeled
    and deveined

½ cup chopped fresh coriander

In saucepan, heat oil over medium heat. Add onion; cook until golden brown, about 6 to 8 minutes. Stir in jalapeño, ginger, and garlic; cook 1 minute more or until jalapeño is soft. Stir in coriander, cumin, garam masala, and turmeric; cook, stirring, for 1 minute or until well blended. Add tomatoes, chicken stock, and lemon juice; cook for 3 to 5 minutes or until sauce is thickened. Add salt. Add shrimp; cover and cook for 5 minutes.

Sprinkle with coriander and serve with basmati rice or naan bread.

Makes about 4 main course servings or 6 appetizer servings.

Roast Pork Shoulder

Jennifer Grange of The Cookbook Store loves this simple, economical dish. Amazingly, no liquid is required; the pork makes its own juices.

3½–4 lb (1.7–2 kg) bone-in pork shoulder

1 tbsp Dijon mustard

½ tsp each: salt and freshly ground black pepper

2 large sprigs rosemary

5 cloves garlic

Preheat oven to 350°F (180°C).

Using a sharp knife, remove skin from pork shoulder and score the fat.

In Dutch oven or large oven-proof saucepan with lid, sear pork over medium heat until it is brown on all sides, about 10 minutes. Remove from heat.

Rub pork with mustard and sprinkle with salt and pepper. Add rosemary and garlic to Dutch oven; cover. Roast in oven for 2½ hours or until meat is almost falling off the bone.

Serve with pan juices and mashed potatoes, if desired.

Makes about 6 servings.

ROSEMARY

Korean Beef Ribs (Kalbi)

From Dr. Julia Lee, a member of FoodShare's board of directors and former board chair. Julia tells us that this recipe always reminds her of the Korean church picnics of her childhood, which featured both barbecued beef ribs and kimchi (the garlicky and spicy fermented cabbage pickle), finished off with copious amounts of watermelon. You will need to seek out a Korean butcher for these thin, bony ribs, which do not resemble spareribs.

2 onions

1 tbsp sesame seeds

¼ cup packed brown sugar

2 tbsp chopped green onions

3 cloves garlic, finely chopped

½ cup soy sauce

¼ cup sesame oil

5 lb (2.2 kg) thinly sliced beef ribs cut across (not through) the bones

Peel onions. Cut in half from tip to root end. Slice crosswise very thinly into half moons. Set aside.

In small frying pan over medium heat, cook sesame seeds for 5 minutes or until golden and fragrant, stirring occasionally.

In bowl, stir together sliced onions, toasted sesame seeds, brown sugar, green onions, garlic, soy sauce, and sesame oil.

Place ribs in 13- × 9-inch (3 L) baking dish. Pour onion mixture over; massage into the beef so all surfaces are soaked. Cover and chill for 4 hours or overnight.

Preheat barbecue to medium heat. Oil grill. Cook ribs in batches for 3 to 4 minutes, turning once.

Serve with rice and Korean condiments.

Makes about 8 servings.

Braised Short Ribs with Chocolate

This dish is inspired by sustainably raised grass-fed beef from Cathy and Bryan Gilvesy at Y U Ranch. Cathy and Bryan have transformed the conversation about economic sustainability for farmers by promoting Alternative Land Use Services (ALUS), a program designed to pay farmers for their environmental stewardship of land and water, allowing them to develop a more sustainable financial and environmental future.

This is a superb version of a hearty meat dish with the rich addition of chocolate and cocoa. Ask your butcher to cut the short ribs thicker than the usual inch or so, for meatier portions. The ribs are best made a day or two ahead and served with mashed potatoes.

¼ cup (about 1 oz/30 g) diced pancetta or bacon

8 pieces (4–5 lb/2 kg) bone-in short ribs

½ tsp salt

½ tsp freshly ground black pepper

1 onion, finely chopped

½ cup diced carrots

½ cup diced celery

3 cloves garlic, finely chopped

2 cups dry red wine

3 cups low-sodium chicken or beef stock

2 cups drained canned diced tomatoes

2 tbsp chopped fresh parsley

1 tsp chopped fresh thyme leaves

2 tbsp grated bittersweet chocolate

1 tbsp cocoa powder

1 tsp finely chopped fresh rosemary

Salt and freshly ground black pepper to taste

Preheat oven to 325°F (160°C).

In Dutch oven or large oven-proof saucepan with lid, cook pancetta over medium heat for 5 minutes or until crisp. Using slotted spoon, transfer to paper towel–lined plate.

Sprinkle ribs with salt and pepper. In batches, cook ribs in same Dutch oven over medium heat, turning occasionally until browned on all sides, about 10 minutes per batch. Transfer to a bowl.

Add onion, carrots, celery, and garlic to Dutch oven; cover and cook over medium heat until soft, stirring occasionally, about 7 minutes. Add wine. Bring to a boil. Boil uncovered, stirring to scrape up browned bits, for 5 minutes or until liquid is reduced by half. Stir in stock, tomatoes, parsley, thyme, and pancetta. Add browned ribs to pan. Bring to a boil. Partially cover and place in oven. Cook for 3 hours or until meat is tender, turning ribs in sauce halfway through cooking time.

Transfer ribs to a plate. Spoon fat from surface of sauce. Bring sauce to a boil; boil until starting to thicken, about 8 minutes. Reduce heat to medium. Stir in chocolate, cocoa, and rosemary until chocolate melts. Add salt and pepper to taste. Return ribs to Dutch oven. Cook over low heat until warmed through.

Makes about 8 servings.

Swiss Chard Rolls

For this clever take on cabbage rolls, the meat filling is baked in advance. A great way to get your greens! The recipe is from Steve Taylor, culinary arts teacher at Bendale Business and Technical Institute in Scarborough, where FoodShare has helped to facilitate Canada's first school market garden so that students learn Food Literacy in all subject areas. At Bendale, the chard used in this recipe comes from garden beds on the former front lawn of the school.

1 tbsp vegetable oil

1 onion, finely chopped

1½ lb (750 g) lean ground beef

1 cup cooked brown rice, cooled

¼ tsp caraway seeds (optional)

½ tsp kosher salt

½ tsp freshly ground black pepper

8 large chard leaves

2 cups tomato sauce (homemade or bottled)

Preheat oven to 350 F (180 C).

In non-stick frying pan, heat oil over medium heat. Cook onion for 10 minutes or until golden and soft, stirring frequently. Cool.

In bowl, stir together beef, rice, caraway seeds (if using), salt, pepper, and cooled onion. Divide mixture into 8 equal balls. Flatten each ball into an oval 3 inches (8 cm) long. Place in large baking dish. Cover with lid or foil. Bake in oven for 30 minutes or until cooked through. Drain off any liquid.

Trim thick stems from Swiss chard leaves so only the part with leaf remains. Turn each leaf flat side down. With knife blade parallel to the leaf surface, trim any thick stalk that juts up above it.

Bring large saucepan of water to gentle simmer over medium heat. Cook chard leaves one at a time for 10 seconds or until just wilted and the thick centre stems are pliable. Plunge immediately into bowl of ice water. Transfer to clean tea towel to dry.

To assemble, place a chard leaf on flat work surface. Place one beef/rice oval on top. Fold right side of leaf over toward centre. Fold left side of leaf over toward centre. Fold ends over to form package. Place seam side down in large clean baking dish. Repeat with remaining leaves and ovals. Pour tomato sauce over rolls. Cover dish.

Bake in centre of oven for 20 minutes or until warmed through (longer if you have refrigerated the filling overnight).

Makes 6 to 8 servings.

I saw the future of food this morning.

SARAH ELTON, SPEAKING ON CBC'S *Here and Now*, ABOUT FOODSHARE'S WORK CREATING TORONTO'S FIRST SCHOOL MARKET GARDEN

share ✳ mains

Spice-Rubbed Steak with Orange Salsa

From Beverley Ann D'Cruz comes this simple steak with an excellent fruit salsa, which she says is "a riff on a recipe from a Martha Stewart magazine." A creative cook, she didn't have that recipe handy when she concocted this one using her own favourite flavours. It's a light, summery meal and even better the next day, when the meat has sat in the juices for some time. Also good eaten cold.

Orange Salsa

2 navel oranges, peeled, segmented, chopped

1 clove garlic, finely chopped

1 green onion, finely chopped

⅓ cup finely chopped fresh coriander

1 tbsp olive oil

Salt and freshly ground black pepper to taste

Steaks

2 boneless rib-eye grilling steaks, ¾ inch (2 cm) thick

1 tsp ground coriander

1 tsp paprika

½ tsp freshly ground black pepper

1 tbsp olive oil

Salt to taste

For orange salsa, in bowl stir together oranges, garlic, green onion, coriander, and oil. Add salt and pepper. Cover and let stand at room temperature while cooking steaks.

Blot steaks dry with paper towel.

In small bowl, stir together coriander, paprika, and pepper. Rub mixture over steaks.

In frying pan, heat oil over medium-high heat. Cook steaks for about 2 minutes per side or until browned on outside but still pink at the centre. Remove steaks from pan; sprinkle with salt. Tent loosely with foil and let stand for 5 minutes.

Slice steak thinly and place on platter. Spoon over orange salsa and its juices.

Makes 2 servings.

Flautas con Carne

When FoodShare first dreamed up our healthy school cafeteria, the Good Food Café, the team from our Field to Table School program wisely suggested engaging the students from the Collège Français who would be using the cafeteria the following year in a "tasting day." One hundred hungry students were divided into groups that moved between five tasting stations, sampling different dishes, writing critiques, and playing a game that ranked dishes according to flavour, presentation, and familiarity.

Flautas was one of the dishes tested that day and one student told us, "Wow! It's like a fiesta in my mouth!" After considering the reviews, Jesús Gomez, FoodShare chef and kitchen co-ordinator, devised this recipe, which is now a Café favourite.

We have learned that familiarity is half the battle when feeding young people. Students are more concerned with how a dish looks (and then how it tastes) than with its contents. If it looks like a taco, no matter what it's filled with, they will gladly eat it.

1 tbsp vegetable oil

1 small onion, thinly sliced

3 cloves garlic, finely chopped

1 lb top sirloin or flank steak, very thinly sliced

4 tomatoes, chopped

2 tsp chili powder

2 tsp Spanish paprika

1 cup tomato juice

1 sweet red or green pepper, thinly sliced

3 leaves Savoy cabbage, thinly sliced

½ cup grated Cheddar cheese

Salt and freshly ground black pepper to taste

4 large (10-inch) flour tortillas

½ cup tomato juice

½ cup grated Cheddar cheese

2 green onions, finely chopped

In large frying pan, heat oil over medium heat. Sauté onion and garlic for 2 to 3 minutes. Add beef, tomatoes, chili powder, paprika, and 1 cup tomato juice. Bring to a boil. Reduce heat, cover, and simmer gently for 30 minutes, stirring occasionally.

Stir in sweet pepper and cabbage. Cover; simmer 10 minutes more or until liquid is reduced and beef is very tender. Add ½ cup Cheddar; season with salt and pepper.

Preheat oven to 350°F (180°C). Cut tortillas in half. Divide and spread filling along the centre of each one and roll up from the rounded side to the flat side.

Pour ½ cup tomato juice in bottom of an 8-inch (2 L) square baking dish and line up flautas on top. Cover with ½ cup Cheddar and green onions. Bake until cheese is melted and flautas are hot, about 5 to 7 minutes.

Makes 4 servings.

Red Meat in Whole Spices (Kata Moshlar Mangsho)

From Nadira Yasmin, a FoodShare student nutrition animator who supports student nutrition programs across the city. Nadira's two children attend Thorncliffe Park Public School, the largest public school in North America, with a student population of over 1,800 representing 47 countries. Nadira has been instrumental in expanding school food programs at Thorncliffe. In 2011, school principal Kevin Battaglia hosted FoodShare's Great Big Crunch, a day of apple-centric Food Literacy activities ending in a synchronized crunch as participants bit into Ontario apples at 2:30 p.m., Eastern Standard Time. Some 112,352 students across Canada crunched their apples with us on that day, too.

This spicy dish can be made with either goat or beef. Its rich taste is enhanced by yogurt. The longer the stew simmers the more tender the meat becomes and it will fall off the bone. Remove any floating bones from the pot before serving.

4 tsp coriander seeds

3 whole dried red chilies

3 tsp black peppercorns

2 tsp cumin seeds

½ cup ghee (clarified butter) or vegetable oil

8 green cardamom pods

8 cloves

2 cinnamon sticks

2 bay leaves

¼ tsp mace or nutmeg

2 cups finely chopped onion

1 head garlic (about 12 cloves), finely chopped

½ cup grated or finely chopped ginger root

1 jalapeño, finely chopped

3½ lb (1.75 kg) goat or beef chuck, cut in 3-inch (8 cm) pieces

2 tsp salt

1½ cups plain yogurt

2 cups chopped tomatoes or canned diced tomatoes, drained

½ cup chopped fresh coriander

In small, dry frying pan over medium heat, toast coriander seeds, red chilies, peppercorns, and cumin seeds until fragrant, about 2 to 3 minutes. Grind into a fine powder. Set aside.

In large saucepan, heat ghee to medium. Add cardamom, cloves, cinnamon, bay leaves, and mace. Toast for 30 seconds. Add onion, garlic, ginger, and jalapeño; sauté for 5 minutes. Add meat, salt, and reserved spices. Sauté until meat is nicely browned, about 10 minutes.

Remove pan from heat and gently stir in yogurt. Return pan to medium-low heat and simmer for 10 minutes. Add tomatoes and 3 cups water. Bring to a boil. Reduce heat and simmer until meat is tender, liquid has reduced, and mixture has thickened, about 1 to 2 hours. Remove bay leaves.

Serve with naan bread or rice, garnished with coriander.

Makes 6 servings.

Butterflied Leg of Lamb with Nectarine Chutney

From Linda Haynes, cookbook author and key supporter of FoodShare over many years. The combination of succulent roast lamb with tangy chutney made of grilled nectarines and onion is simply super. Leave the core of the onion intact when cutting wedges so it doesn't fall apart when you grill it.

2 lb (1 kg) butterflied leg of lamb

3 cloves garlic, finely chopped

1½ tsp dried mint

1 tbsp finely chopped fresh oregano

2 tbsp olive oil

¼ tsp freshly ground black pepper

½ tsp salt

Chutney

1 sweet white onion (e.g., Vidalia), cut in wedges

5 nectarines (skin on), pitted and quartered

2 tbsp olive oil

1 tsp sherry vinegar

⅓ cup red wine vinegar

¼ cup granulated sugar

1 tbsp finely chopped fresh oregano

½ tsp freshly ground black pepper

1 sprig fresh mint

1 tbsp finely chopped fresh mint

Place lamb, fat side up, in shallow baking dish.

In small bowl, combine garlic, dried mint, oregano, oil, and pepper. Massage mixture all over lamb. Cover with plastic wrap. Marinate for 45 minutes at room temperature or for up to 10 hours in the fridge.

Preheat oven to 425°F (220°C).

For chutney, toss together onion, nectarines, and oil. On barbecue preheated to medium-high or in grill pan on stovetop, grill onion and nectarines in batches until nicely charred but not cooked through. Add to bowl with sherry vinegar; toss to coat. Roughly chop mixture. Place in 8-inch (2 L) square baking dish. Stir in red wine vinegar, sugar, oregano, pepper, and mint sprig. Bake uncovered in centre of oven for 30 minutes. Cool to room temperature. Remove mint sprig and stir in chopped mint.

Transfer lamb to roasting pan. Sprinkle with salt. Roast, fat side up, for 20 to 30 minutes or until meat thermometer reads 145°F (63°C) for medium-rare or 160°F (71°C) for medium. Let lamb rest 5 minutes before slicing.

Serve with chutney.

Make about 6 servings.

Somali Lamb Stew

This recipe comes from Marian Yusuf, Toronto Public Health nutritionist, who has modified it by adding more vegetables. Marian has been an invaluable partner to FoodShare and has worked with us on many projects over the years, supporting our student and baby nutrition programs, linking FoodShare to the City's successful peer nutrition program, and most recently working as a member of the Toronto Public Health Food Strategy team to advance community food animation and a mobile produce-vending pilot.

2 tbsp vegetable oil

4 cloves garlic, finely chopped

1 cup chopped onion

1½ lb (750 g) boneless lamb, cut in 1-inch (2.5 cm) pieces

2 Yukon Gold potatoes, peeled and cut in 1-inch (2.5 cm) pieces

4 carrots, cut in 1-inch (2.5 cm) pieces

1 can (28 oz/796 mL) diced tomatoes

1 tbsp ground cumin

1 small red chili

2 cups low-sodium chicken stock or water

10 asparagus spears, trimmed and cut in 1-inch (2.5 cm) pieces

1 cup chopped sweet red or green pepper

½ cup chopped fresh coriander

Salt and freshly ground black pepper to taste

Lemon (optional)

In large saucepan, heat oil over medium heat. Add garlic and onion; sauté for 5 minutes. Add lamb; cook for 10 minutes or until browned.

Add potatoes, carrots, tomatoes and their juice, cumin, chili, and stock. Bring to a boil. Reduce heat and simmer uncovered for 30 minutes or until meat and potatoes are tender and mixture is thickened.

Add asparagus, pepper, and half the coriander; cook for 5 minutes. Add salt and pepper.

Serve hot over brown basmati rice or with whole-grain pita bread, garnished with remaining coriander and a squeeze of lemon, if using.

Makes 6 servings.

Food Policy:
Foodshare's Three Recommendations for Three Levels of Government

FEDERAL POLICIES

National child and student nutrition program

The federal government needs to work with the provinces to implement a universal student nutrition program and children's nutrition programs that will encourage young people to eat healthy local food at school and at home.

Strong social safety net to reduce hunger

Programs are needed to make sure that provinces invest in housing, child care, food, health care, and dental care. (Bring back the Canada Assistance Plan, a social safety net below which no citizen can fall.)

Ministry of food security

A ministry is needed to ensure that every Canadian is able to eat well each day and to determine how we could grow enough food nationally to feed our population.

PROVINCIAL POLICIES

Universal student nutrition program

All children in all communities need access to at least one healthy snack at school. The province should extend funding beyond the current levels for student nutrition programs to implement a universal program and integrate Food Literacy throughout the school day.

Support to local farmers

The province should support Alternative Land Use Services (ALUS) tax incentives that support farmers who use sustainable growing practices, and should explore developing other creative programs to support farmers who grow food for local consumption.

Good Food Box programs

Ontario should support Good Food Box programs in every community to help improve access to healthy food and increase market share for farmers.

CITY POLICIES

Public food on public land

Parks and Recreation departments should develop community-friendly policies that make it easy for neighbourhood groups to develop gardens, produce markets, and farmers' markets.

Every school a healthy food centre

Every child in every city should have a school program that encourages healthy eating and food growing.

Every social housing building a local food culture

Cities should work with senior levels of government on making all social housing buildings sites of fabulous food systems—composting, food growing, and more.

desserts

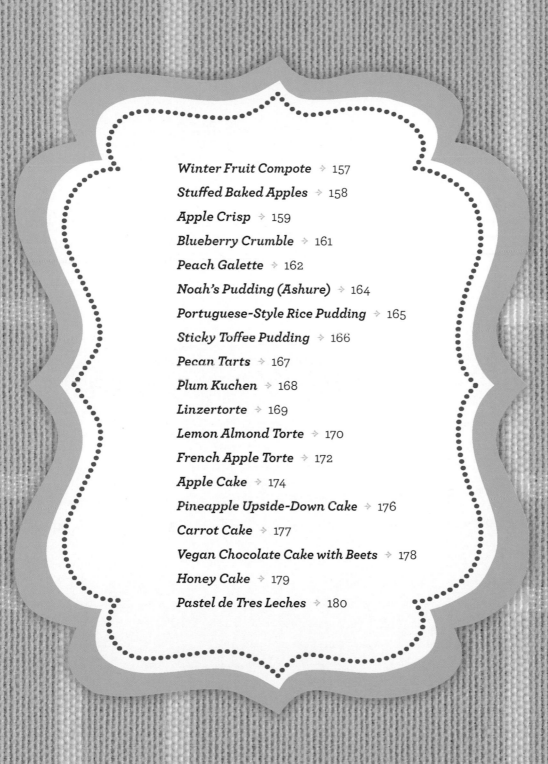

leadership

"Bread and roses" was the rallying cry of immigrant women workers in Lawrence, Massachusetts, in 1912 on strike against lower wages. They were a social union, striking for the rights of all workers. To be alive, they argued, was to need beauty, symbolized by the rose, as well as the necessities of life, symbolized by bread. "Yes, we fight for bread, but we fight for roses, too," was the refrain of their song.

Since our formation, FoodShare has worked for a world beyond hunger, in which everyone has access to enough healthy, beautiful food and farmers are paid fairly for the food they produce. Influenced by the work of Frances Moore Lappé the people who organized the movement for FoodShare, Stuart Coles and Jennifer Welsh, understood that hunger is a problem of distribution, not of production.

We freely share tools, resources, policies, and programs with everyone who can benefit from them, taking an open-source approach that honours the fact that we are all part of a movement working for change and for a just food system. Our staff of experts—every one a passionate food security community development worker and educator—support and mentor communities in drawing on their own strengths to adapt the solutions we offer and take them further. FoodShare works quite literally from field to table, taking a multifaceted and long-term view of hunger and food issues and working to empower through food-based initiatives while advocating for the broader public policies needed to ensure that everyone has adequate access to sustainably produced, good healthy food.

Each week we answer calls and emails and host visits from across the province, the country, and the world from those who seek our advice to start programs in their own communities. Through our manuals, website, and this support, we provide replicable models and have helped start hundreds of programs, reaching tens of thousands of people.

When Luiz Inácio Lula da Silva gave his inaugural speech as president of Brazil in 2003, he was the first global leader to commit his government to ending hunger. Lula had been hungry as a child and, he said, hunger could be stopped. Though there is much to be done, Brazil's Fome Zero (Zero Hunger) initiatives have made a real difference. Like Lula, the garment workers of Lawrence, Frances Moore Lappé, Stuart Coles, and Jennifer Welsh, we at FoodShare know that it is important to fight for roses while we fight for bread.

So here, from many joyful kitchens to yours, is a cornucopia of desserts to inspire us all to have beauty in our lives as we work for social justice. Yes we fight for Sukuma Wiki (Kenyan kale), but we fight for apple crumble, too!

Winter Fruit Compote

A fabulous dinner party dessert to serve with cookies, cake and ice cream, or custard. Use whatever dried fruits take your fancy, although this version with figs and prunes is top notch. Cut the fresh fruit in uniform chunks (about ¾ inch/2 cm works well) so they cook at similar rates.

1 cup unsweetened fruit juice (apple, pineapple, or orange)

½ cup port wine

12 pitted prunes, cut in chunks

6 dried figs, cut in chunks

2 apples, cored, peeled, cut in chunks

2 Bosc pears, cored, peeled, cut in chunks

1 package (10 oz/300 g) frozen berries, thawed

In large heavy-bottomed saucepan, combine fruit juice, port, prunes, and figs. Bring to a boil. Reduce heat to low and simmer uncovered for 5 minutes. Using slotted spoon, transfer prunes and figs to glass serving bowl.

Add apples and pears to liquid in saucepan. Bring to a boil. Reduce heat to low, cover, and simmer for 4 to 6 minutes or until fruit barely begins to turn soft. Add mixture to the prunes and figs in bowl.

Cool to room temperature. Stir in thawed berries and their juice. Chill.

Serve with ice cream, sweetened plain yogurt, or custard.

Makes 8 to 10 servings.

Our school participated in The Great Big Crunch! and it was awesome. Can you believe that I had a student who had never tasted an apple before, nor eaten fresh food? He ate a slice, liked it, and asked for seconds. Now his homework consists of eating a fresh fruit or vegetable 3 times a week. Yahoo!

A TORONTO PRIMARY SCHOOL TEACHER

Stuffed Baked Apples

This is a terrific version of an old-fashioned standby, contributed by a group of corporate volunteers who visited FoodShare to help us pack Good Food Boxes.

**4 large baking apples
(e.g., Ida Red,
Cortland, McIntosh)**

2 tsp fresh lemon juice

**1 cup finely chopped
pitted prunes**

**¼ cup finely chopped
walnuts**

3 tbsp liquid honey

½ tsp cinnamon

½ cup orange juice

Preheat oven to 325°F (160°C).

Use a melon baller to core apples. Start at the stem end and scoop down into the flesh, pulling up core and seeds and hollowing out the apple without breaking through the sides or the bottom. Rub exposed apple flesh with lemon juice. Using fork, prick top of each apple several times.

In small bowl, stir together prunes, walnuts, honey, and cinnamon. Stuff one-quarter of mixture into each apple, mounding it on top if necessary. Set in 9-inch (2.5 L) square baking dish or shallow casserole dish.

Whisk together orange juice and ⅔ cup water. Pour over apples. Bake uncovered in centre of oven, basting occasionally with pan juices, for 30 to 40 minutes or until tender when pierced with tip of a knife.

Cool slightly before serving with custard, ice cream, or whipped cream.

Makes 4 servings.

Good Hea

Apple Crisp

Marion Kane makes this regularly with local fruit in season. Northern Spys, available in late fall, are best but the addition of lemon juice and/or cranberries to Cortland, Mutsu, or Royal Gala apples can achieve the tartness crucial for contrast with the sweet topping. This can also be made with plums, peaches or, best of all, a mixture of fruit. It's great made with rhubarb, but add more sugar to the fruit layer. An earthenware baking dish works well and is attractive for serving. The topping is tops: a crunchy, crisp, cookie-like sensation.

¾ **cup all-purpose flour**

¾ **cup large-flake or quick-cooking (not instant) rolled oats**

¾ **cup packed brown sugar**

¾ **cup cold butter, cubed**

½ **tsp cinnamon**

4–5 **tart apples, cored, peeled, sliced**

Preheat oven to 375°F (190°C). Lightly butter medium baking dish, 8 inches (2 L) square or equivalent size.

In large bowl, combine flour, oats, and brown sugar. Add butter; using pastry blender or two knives, cut it in until mixture resembles coarse crumbs. Rub between fingers until butter is soft and mixture begins to form a ball. It will resemble cookie dough in texture.

Arrange apple slices in prepared dish. Sprinkle with cinnamon. Use hands to shape oat mixture to cover apples evenly. Bake in centre of oven about 40 to 50 minutes or until browned on top, apples are soft, and juices bubble up.

Serve warm with ice cream.

Makes about 6 servings.

The Norfolk Fruit Growers' Association in Simcoe, the oldest farm co-operative in Ontario, delivers millions of apples a year to Food-Share's Field to Table Community Food Hub. Together we have developed a special 10 lb/5 kg bag of pre-washed apples that can be easily carried into a class and served. Each contains 50 small apples and through our subsidized distribution system can be purchased by a student nutrition program for under $3. These child-friendly apples used to be left in the field, sold for juice, or exported, as it was thought there was no market in Canada.

Blueberry Crumble

Joseph and Serena LeBlanc of True North Community Co-operative, based in Thunder Bay, Ontario, sent along this family recipe for blueberry crumble. Joseph is the community project co-ordinator at Nishnawbe Aski Nation, the political territorial organization representing 49 First Nation communities in northern Ontario. Though FoodShare delivers food only in the Toronto area, we could not turn down his request to get more affordable produce to the Fort Albany First Nation in collaboration with True North. We started a pilot project in 2011, and it has proven to be an affordable means of sourcing and distributing foods.

6 cups fresh or frozen wild blueberries

1 tsp cinnamon

1 tsp fresh lemon juice

1 cup quick-cooking rolled oats

¾ cup all-purpose flour

¾ cup firmly packed brown sugar

½ cup softened butter

Heat oven to 375°F (190°C).

Place berries in ungreased 11- × 7-inch (2 L) casserole dish. Sprinkle with cinnamon, 1 tablespoon water, and lemon juice.

In large bowl, combine oats, flour, sugar, and butter; mix with pastry blender or fork until crumbly. Sprinkle crumb mixture evenly over berries.

Bake in centre of oven for 25 to 30 minutes or until topping is golden brown and blueberries are bubbling. Let rest for 10 minutes before serving.

Serve crumble warm with vanilla ice cream or fresh whipped cream, if desired.

Makes 6 to 8 servings.

The Nishnawbe Aski Nation (NAN) encompasses James Bay Treaty No. 9 and the Ontario portion of Treaty No. 5, with a land mass covering two-thirds of the province of Ontario. Members in Fort Albany are now able to order food as if they were Good Food Market co-ordinators in Toronto, and True North has the food picked up by a truck with a refrigerated trailer from FoodShare and driven to Cochrane, Ontario, where it is loaded on the Ontario Northland freight train and shipped to Moosonee, Ontario. From there the food is flown into Fort Albany First Nation and distributed through Good Food Boxes and an alternative market.

Peach Galette

Created by Marion Kane as she was working on this book, this luscious dessert has become a new favourite. For dough, use all butter and omit lard, if desired. You can use any tender fruit for this: plums, apricots, nectarines, or cherries. Local fruit in season is best. If using plums or apricots, double the amount of sugar in the filling. You can peel peaches by the old-fashioned method—plunging them in boiling water for a minute or two—or buy one of the excellent serrated peelers now available. The latter method is easier and prevents the peaches from leaking juice. This makes a large pie—enough for a crowd and ideal for a summer gathering.

Pie Dough

2 cups all-purpose flour

2 tbsp granulated sugar

¾ cup cold butter, cubed

¼ cup cold lard

6 to 8 tbsp ice water

Almond Layer

½ cup ground almonds

2 tbsp all-purpose flour

2 tbsp light brown or organic cane sugar

Peach Filling

6 cups sliced, pitted, peeled ripe peaches (about 8)

3 tbsp light brown or organic cane sugar

3 tbsp all-purpose flour

1 tbsp fresh lemon juice

Glaze and Garnish

1 egg, beaten with a little milk

1 tbsp granulated sugar

¼ cup peach, apricot, or apple jelly, melted

About ½ cup sliced almonds, toasted

For pie dough, combine flour and sugar in food processor. Add butter; pulse on and off 5 or 6 times. Add lard; pulse on and off a few times or until mixture resembles coarse crumbs. Gradually add ice water until mixture begins to clump. Form dough into ball; wrap in plastic wrap and chill about 1 hour.

Preheat oven to 400°F (200°C).

For almond layer, in small bowl combine almonds, flour, and sugar.

For peach filling, in large bowl combine peaches, sugar, flour, and lemon juice.

Roll out pie dough on floured surface to about 15 inches (38 cm) in diameter. Place on large pizza pan or other baking pan. Spread almond layer mixture evenly over dough. Mound peach filling in middle of dough, leaving about 2 inches (5 cm) clear around the edge. Fold the dough border over peaches, pleating at intervals. (A large centre section of filling will not be covered.) Brush edges of dough with egg mixture, then sprinkle with sugar.

Bake in centre of oven about 40 to 50 minutes or until pie is golden brown. Cool to room temperature.

Spread melted jelly over peaches with pastry brush. Sprinkle with toasted almonds. (To toast almonds, cook in dry frying pan over low heat about 5 minutes or until golden brown.)

Serve with ice cream, thickened yogurt (strained overnight through cheesecloth), or crème fraîche.

Makes 8 to 12 servings.

Torrie Warner, whose grandfather established Warners Farm in 1919, describes the mutual benefits of the new food system being created by FoodShare and local farmers.

"Warners Farm produces mainly tree fruit and grapes in Beamsville. The closure of the grape juice plant in St. Catharines, and the following year the closure of the canning factory in St. Davids, was particularly difficult. Eighteen acres of grapes and 10 acres of tree fruit were removed, forcing us to look for alternative avenues to sell our fruit. FoodShare is one of our new customers. This relationship started in 2009, and has developed into a weekly delivery during the season. FoodShare purchases peaches, plums, apricots, and grapes from us and is a valued customer. The order is usually received Friday; the fruit is harvested and packed on the weekend and is delivered Monday. This seems to be working well."

Noah's Pudding (Ashure)

Food democracy leader Mustafa Koç, founding member (with FoodShare's Debbie Field) of Food Secure Canada and a sociology professor at Ryerson University, contributed this unusual, nutritious, and tasty dairy-free Turkish dessert, also called ashure. The biblical Noah purportedly made this with his remaining stores when the ark lodged on Mount Ararat after the flood. Substitute wheatberries for barley if you like and use any dried fruit, such as figs or dates. Garnish with chopped nuts and/or a bit of cream. This could also be a breakfast cereal. Rosewater is sold in Middle Eastern food shops and some supermarkets.

½ cup chopped dried apricots

½ cup currants

½ cup raisins

1 cup pearl barley, rinsed and drained

¼ cup short-grain rice, rinsed and drained

1 can (14 oz/398 mL) chickpeas or navy beans, rinsed and drained

2 cups granulated sugar

¼ cup rice flour

¼ cup rosewater

Place apricots, currants, and raisins in bowl; add boiling water to cover. Let soak for 5 minutes. Drain and set aside.

In large heavy-bottomed saucepan, combine barley and 4 cups water. Bring to a boil. Reduce heat to medium-low, cover, and cook for 45 minutes or until barley is tender. Stir in 8 cups water, rice, beans, and drained dried fruit. Bring to a boil. Reduce heat to low and simmer uncovered for 10 minutes, stirring often. Slowly add sugar, stirring constantly.

In small bowl, stir rice flour with ¼ cup water to make a paste; stir into pudding. Cook, stirring frequently, for 10 minutes or until thickened.

Remove from heat; stir in rosewater. Transfer to large serving bowl or small individual serving bowls. Chill.

Makes about 12 servings.

Portuguese-Style Rice Pudding

Adapted from a recipe by Mario Silva, former member of parliament for Davenport and a great neighbour to FoodShare since our Field to Table Community Food Hub is in his area. Use a vegetable peeler to get long strips of yellow rind from a scrubbed lemon, leaving the white pith behind. Use ⅓ cup sugar for a less sweet version. A little of this rich dessert goes a long way. Serve with fruit salad or compote, if desired.

½ cup arborio rice
4 cups whole milk
½ cup granulated sugar
¼ tsp salt
5 strips lemon rind
1 tsp vanilla extract
3 egg yolks
Cinnamon

In large heavy-bottomed saucepan, combine rice, milk, sugar, salt, and lemon rind. Bring to a boil. Reduce heat to medium-low, cover, and cook for 50 minutes, stirring occasionally.

Turn off heat. Remove rind. Stir in vanilla. Beat egg yolks in small bowl and quickly stir into rice pudding. Let stand, covered, for 10 minutes.

Serve warm, sprinkled with cinnamon.

Makes about 6 servings.

This is revolutionary!
A GRADE 3 STUDENT DURING
FOODSHARE'S GREAT BIG CRUNCH

Sticky Toffee Pudding

Marion Kane came up with this version of a brilliant dessert with help from top Toronto pastry chef and good friend Joanne Yolles. The trick is pouring the hot toffee sauce over the still-warm cake.

Pudding

3 tbsp strong coffee

1 tbsp brandy, Scotch, or rum

1 cup coarsely chopped pitted dried dates

1 cup all-purpose flour

1 tsp baking powder

1 tsp baking soda

¼ tsp cinnamon

Pinch salt

½ cup packed dark brown sugar

¼ cup butter, softened

1 egg

1 tsp vanilla extract

Toffee Sauce

¾ cup packed dark brown sugar

¾ cup whipping cream

6 tbsp butter

Preheat oven to 350°F (180°C). Grease 8-inch (2 L) square metal cake pan and line bottom with parchment paper.

For pudding, in small saucepan, bring coffee, brandy, and 1 cup water to a boil. Add dates; stir well. Remove from heat.

In small bowl, combine flour, baking powder, baking soda, cinnamon, and salt. In another bowl and using electric mixer, beat sugar with butter until fluffy; beat in egg and vanilla.

In food processor, pulse dates with their liquid briefly just until chunky, not smooth.

Using wooden spoon, stir flour mixture and date mixture alternately into butter mixture, making three additions of flour and two of dates. Pour into prepared pan.

Bake in centre of oven for 25 to 30 minutes or until browned and springy to the touch, and tester inserted in centre comes out clean.

Meanwhile, for toffee sauce, in small saucepan cook sugar, whipping cream, and butter over medium heat, stirring frequently, for 7 minutes or until smooth, slightly thickened, and simmering.

When pudding comes out of the oven, poke holes in top using skewers. Slowly pour about half of toffee sauce over top, reserving the remainder.

Serve warm with vanilla ice cream, whipped cream, or crème fraîche, if desired, and with reserved warmed toffee sauce.

Makes about 8 servings.

Pecan Tarts

From David Tilson, member of parliament for Dufferin-Caledon, come these excellent little tarts, known in his family as the famous Tilson Tarts. MP Tilson has twice visited FoodShare to announce federal youth employment funding connected to our Focus on Food youth intern program.

The pastry is an easy, press-in version: no rolling involved. Use a little less salt in the filling, if desired.

3 oz (90 g) cream cheese, softened

½ cup butter, softened

1 cup all-purpose flour

1 cup finely chopped pecans

¾ cup packed brown sugar

1 tbsp melted butter

1 egg, beaten

1 tsp vanilla extract

¼ tsp salt

In bowl and using electric mixer, beat cream cheese with butter until blended. Add flour; beat until soft dough forms. Chill for at least 30 minutes to firm dough up.

Preheat oven to 350°F (180°C).

Roll dough by tablespoons into balls; you should get 24. Press one ball of dough into each cup of two 12-cup standard muffin pans, pressing evenly over bottom and about ½ inch (1 cm) up sides.

In bowl, stir together pecans, brown sugar, melted butter, egg, vanilla, and salt. Divide mixture evenly among muffin cups, about a scant tablespoon in each cup.

Bake in centre of oven for 20 to 25 minutes or until golden. Cool in pans.

Makes 24 tarts.

Plum Kuchen

Ulla Knowles, a manager in FoodShare's student nutrition program, sent along this classic German kuchen, a delectable tart-cum-cake that's easy to make. Use nectarines, peaches, cherries, or a combination of tender fruit instead of plums, if desired.

Ulla, a geologist by training, started a morning snack program at St. Theresa Catholic School in Etobicoke in 1996, staying involved as her three children moved up through primary school. Student nutrition programs in Toronto are supported by the Toronto Partners for Student Nutrition, which includes Toronto Public Health, the Toronto District School Board, the Toronto Catholic District School Board, the Angel Foundation for Learning, the Toronto Foundation for Student Success, and community groups like FoodShare.

2 cups all-purpose flour

¾ cup granulated sugar

2½ tsp baking powder

½ cup cold butter, cut in cubes

2 eggs, beaten

2½ lb (1.25 kg) ripe plums (about 12 large plums, more if using prune plums)

¼ cup granulated sugar

1 tbsp cinnamon

2 tbsp cold butter, cut in cubes

Preheat oven to 325°F (160°C). Grease 13- × 9-inch (3.5 L) metal cake pan.

Place flour, ¾ cup sugar, and baking powder in food processor. Process to combine. Add ½ cup butter; pulse on and off until mixture resembles coarse crumbs. Add eggs; pulse on and off until mixture clumps. Pat mixture evenly into bottom of prepared cake pan.

Cut plums in half and pit them. In bowl, toss plums with ¼ cup sugar and cinnamon. Place closely together in rows on top of dough, alternating rows cut side up and cut side down. Dot with 2 tablespoons butter.

Bake in centre of oven for 30 to 40 minutes or until cake is brown around edges and cooked through at centre. Cool in pan.

Serve with lightly sweetened whipped cream, if desired. Best eaten within 24 hours of baking. Store at room temperature.

Makes about 12 servings.

Linzertorte

This is from Marion Kane's mother, Ruth Schachter, who is a whiz at European baking. It's her trademark dessert and looks as good as it tastes. Once you've tried this, you'll never look back.

1¼ cups whole unblanched almonds (skin on)

¾ cup butter, softened

½ cup granulated sugar

2 egg yolks

1 tsp finely grated lemon rind

1 tbsp fresh lemon juice

1 cup all-purpose flour

1 tbsp cocoa powder

½ tsp cinnamon

Pinch ground cloves

About 1 cup good-quality raspberry jam

1 egg white

Icing sugar

Place almonds in food processor; pulse on and off just until ground.

In large bowl and using electric mixer, cream butter and sugar until fluffy. Add egg yolks, lemon rind, and lemon juice. Beat until smooth.

In another bowl, combine flour, cocoa, cinnamon, cloves, and ground almonds. Stir into butter mixture to form soft dough. Gather into ball, wrap in plastic wrap, and refrigerate at least 1 hour or overnight. (If chilling overnight, bring to room temperature 30 minutes before using.)

Preheat oven to 350°F (180°C).

With floured hands, evenly pat two-thirds of dough onto bottom and up sides of 9-inch (2.5 L) springform pan or fluted flan ring with removable bottom. Carefully spread jam over dough.

On floured surface, roll remaining dough into oval ¼ inch (5 mm) thick. Cut into strips ¾ inch (2 cm) wide; arrange in lattice pattern on top of jam, pressing edges into edge of torte. (If strips break, simply press them back together.)

In small bowl, lightly beat egg white. Brush onto lattice strips and edges of torte.

Bake in centre of oven 45 to 50 minutes or until pastry is a dark, rich brown. Cool completely in pan on rack. Remove side of pan. Dust with icing sugar before cutting in narrow wedges.

Serve with vanilla ice cream, sweetened plain yogurt, or crème fraîche.

Makes about 10 servings.

Lemon Almond Torte

Jennifer Welsh, first co-ordinator of the Centre for Studies in Food Security at Ryerson University and an important leader of the early years of the food security movement in Canada, offers a version of this elegant lemon torte, her signature dessert. The delicate sponge cake is topped with paper-thin lemon slices and a sweet meringue topping. Jennifer tells us she substitutes potato starch for the flour during Passover. You can bake the cake layer ahead of time.

4 eggs, separated

¾ cup granulated sugar

2 tsp finely grated lemon rind

1 cup ground almonds

1 tbsp all-purpose flour

2 pinches granulated sugar

2 lemons

3 egg whites

¼ cup granulated sugar

¾ cup ground almonds

Icing sugar

Preheat oven to 350°F (180°C). Butter 9-inch (2.5 L) springform pan.

In large bowl and using electric mixer, beat egg yolks with ¾ cup sugar until thick and pale yellow, about 4 minutes. Stir in lemon rind, 1 cup almonds, and flour.

In another bowl and using clean beaters, beat 4 egg whites on low speed until foamy. Add 2 pinches of sugar; increase speed and beat until stiff, shiny peaks form. Stir quarter of egg white mixture into yolk mixture. Fold in remaining beaten whites. Pour batter into prepared pan, smoothing top.

Bake in centre of oven until browned and cake starts to shrink from side of pan, about 18 to 25 minutes. Leave oven on. Remove cake and cool to room temperature in pan on wire rack. Cake will shrink more as it cools.

Scrub lemons. With sharp knife, slice crosswise into paper-thin slices. Poke out seeds. Place slices flat on cutting board; cut rind, pith, and membrane from outer edge of each slice. Leaving cooled cake in pan, arrange lemon slices over top.

In bowl and using electric mixer, beat 3 egg whites until soft peaks form. Gradually add ¼ cup sugar, continuing to beat until stiff peaks form. Fold in ¾ cup almonds. Leaving cake in pan and using spatula dipped in cold water, spread mixture over cake, to edge of pan. Bake in centre of oven until meringue is golden brown, about 15 to 20 minutes. Cool to room temperature in pan on wire rack. Remove side of pan.

Serve at room temperature dusted with sifted icing sugar and, if desired, drizzled with raspberry coulis.

Makes about 8 servings.

French Apple Torte

From Marion Kane, whose mother found an initial version in an old cookbook by British author Elizabeth David and often bakes it for birthdays or afternoon tea. An old-school baker, Marion's mother makes the dough for the torte layers by hand, but this recipe brings the ease of a food processor. A dainty little cake, it is easy to make. It took a couple of phone calls to her mother in the UK for Marion to perfect this. Northern Spy, available in late fall, is her favourite apple for this. Not-too-sweet varieties like Ida Red, Cortland, Macs, and Mutsu—or a combination—are second best.

Applesauce

4 large tart apples, cored, peeled, sliced
1 tbsp fresh lemon juice

Torte Layers

1½ cups all-purpose flour
½ cup icing sugar
½ cup salted butter, softened
2 egg yolks
½ tsp vanilla extract

Icing

½ cup icing sugar
1 tbsp orange juice

Garnish

¼ cup sliced almonds

Preheat oven to 350°F (180°C).

For applesauce, lightly butter casserole dish. Add sliced apples and lemon juice; toss to combine. Bake covered in oven for 30 minutes or until apples are very tender and start to break down. Remove from oven. Stir mixture to form applesauce. Cool. Leave oven on.

For garnish, place almonds on rimmed baking sheet. Bake in centre of oven for 4 to 5 minutes or until golden and fragrant. Set aside.

For torte layers, place flour, sugar, and butter in food processor. Pulse on and off until mixture resembles coarse crumbs. Add egg yolks and vanilla; process just until dough begins to clump. Turn dough out onto lightly floured surface. Shape into ball. Divide into 3 equal pieces; flatten into discs. Wrap each disc in plastic wrap. Refrigerate about 30 minutes.

Preheat oven to 325°F (160°C).

Line 3 rimmed baking sheets with parchment paper. Using 8-inch round (1.2 L) cake pan, trace an 8-inch (20 cm) round on each piece of parchment. Transfer a piece of parchment to work surface. Place a dough disc in centre of circle. Roll to fill circle. Edges do not need to be perfect. Return to baking sheet. Bake in centre of oven for 15 to 20 minutes or until golden brown. Meanwhile, roll out another dough disc. Continue baking, rolling out next layer while previous one bakes. Cool layers completely. Gently peel off paper.

For icing, in small bowl stir together icing sugar and orange juice.

To assemble, place a torte layer on cake plate. Using spatula, spread with half the applesauce. Repeat layers. Top with third torte layer. Spread with icing. Sprinkle with toasted almonds. Cut with sharp knife to serve.

Makes 8 servings.

*share * desserts*

Apple Cake

This terrific recipe comes from Linda Briskin, a long-time union and social activist who teaches at York University and has written extensively on the history and struggles of union women. The recipe was handed down by Linda's aunt and is a traditional eastern European dessert that's stood the test of time. Tart apples, especially Northern Spy, are ideal. You can also use pears, plums, cherries, blueberries, and strawberries in season and increase sugar in cake batter to 1 cup if you prefer a sweeter cake, or substitute brown sugar for granulated.

Cake

⅔ **cup vegetable oil**

3 **eggs**

½ **cup granulated sugar**

1 **tsp vanilla extract**

1½ **cups all-purpose flour**

2 **tsp baking powder**

½ **tsp salt**

Filling

6 **tart apples (e.g., Northern Spy, Cortland), cored, peeled, coarsely chopped**

½ **cup packed brown sugar**

2 **tbsp all-purpose flour**

1 **tbsp fresh lemon juice**

2 **tsp cinnamon**

Preheat oven to 350°F (180°C). Grease 9-inch (2.5 L) square metal cake pan.

In bowl and using electric mixer, beat oil, eggs, sugar, and vanilla until creamy. In another bowl, stir together flour, baking power, and salt. With wooden spoon, stir into oil mixture.

For filling, in bowl, combine apples, brown sugar, flour, lemon juice, and cinnamon.

Spread three-quarters of cake batter into prepared cake pan. Top with filling. Smooth remaining cake batter over filling.

Bake in centre of oven for 50 to 60 minutes or until cake is golden brown. Cool in pan on rack. Cut into squares to serve.

Make about 16 servings.

Pineapple Upside-Down Cake

A favourite that has become a signature dish for Good Food Box customer service co-ordinator Delsie Hyatt, who is asked for this recipe again and again. Delsie works directly with the volunteer co-ordinators of over 200 community drop-offs, where neighbours gather across Toronto to pick up their Good Food Boxes. Off the top of her head, she can give the history of every single co-ordinator and volunteer who helps us pack the boxes and is the proud recipient of wonderful weekly stories of potlucks and recipe sharing. This makes a shallow cake, great served with vanilla ice cream.

3 tbsp butter

½ cup packed brown sugar

1 can (14 oz/398 mL) pineapple slices

4 maraschino cherries, cut in half

⅓ cup butter, softened

½ cup granulated sugar

1 egg

1 tsp vanilla extract

1 cup all-purpose flour

1¼ tsp baking powder

¼ tsp salt

Whipped cream (optional)

Preheat oven to 350°F (180°C).

Place 3 tablespoons butter in 9-inch (2.5 L) square metal cake pan. Heat in oven until butter is melted. Remove pan from oven. Stir in brown sugar until well combined.

Drain pineapple, reserving ½ cup juice; use remainder for another purpose. Arrange pineapple slices in bottom of cake pan. Place half a cherry in middle of each pineapple slice.

In bowl and using electric mixer, beat ⅓ cup butter with granulated sugar until fluffy. Beat in egg and vanilla. Add flour, baking powder, salt, and reserved pineapple juice; beat until combined. Spread over top of pineapple in baking dish.

Bake in centre of oven for 35 to 40 minutes or until tester inserted in centre comes out clean. Cool for 5 minutes in pan, then carefully invert onto a cake plate.

Serve warm with dollop of whipped cream or scoop of ice cream.

Makes about 9 servings.

Carrot Cake

From FoodShare's Sybil Pinnock, baker extraordinaire, dancing machine, and co-ordinator of our popular Field to Table Catering, comes this tasty classic. Use the large holes on a box grater to shred the carrots. Don't use fine coconut for this or the texture will be wrong.

Cake

2 cups shredded carrots

1½ cups all-purpose flour

1½ cups granulated sugar

2 tsp cinnamon

½ tsp salt

½ tsp baking soda

¾ cup vegetable oil

2 eggs, beaten

2 tsp vanilla extract

1 cup canned crushed pineapple or fresh pineapple, finely chopped

¾ cup chopped pecans

¾ cup unsweetened medium-shredded coconut

Icing

1½ cups icing sugar

4 oz (125 g) cream cheese, softened

3 tbsp unsalted butter, softened

1 tbsp fresh lemon juice

½ tsp vanilla extract

Garnish

½ cup unsweetened medium-shredded coconut

Place carrots in small saucepan. Add cold water to cover. Bring to a boil. Cook for 4 minutes or until tender. Drain and set aside.

Preheat oven to 350°F (180°C). Grease 10-inch (3 L) springform pan.

Into large bowl, sift together flour, sugar, cinnamon, salt, and baking soda.

In another bowl, whisk together oil, eggs, and vanilla. Using electric mixer, beat into dry ingredients just until moistened. Using rubber spatula, fold in pineapple, pecans, coconut, and cooled carrots. Pour into prepared pan; smooth top.

Bake in centre of oven for 50 minutes or until tester inserted in centre of cake comes out clean. Cool in pan on wire rack for 10 minutes, leaving oven on.

For garnish, place coconut on rimmed baking sheet; toast in oven for 5 minutes or until golden and fragrant. Set aside.

Remove side of springform pan. Take cake off pan bottom; cool on rack to room temperature.

For icing, sift icing sugar; set aside. In bowl and using electric mixer, cream together cream cheese and butter. Beat in icing sugar, lemon juice, and vanilla until smooth. Cover top and side of cake with icing. Sprinkle toasted coconut over top of cake.

Makes about 10 servings.

Vegan Chocolate Cake with Beets

Despite its lack of butter and eggs, this is a surprisingly rich cake. It costs pennies to make (good-quality cocoa powder and real vanilla are the only indulgences) and is almost as simple as purchasing a mix. Grated beets add moisture and nutrients, but we've also made the cake with zucchini, carrots, blueberries, mangoes, apples, bananas, and chocolate chips— whatever is on hand. It is a most forgiving recipe.

This version was passed on by two student nutrition organizers. Fiona Bowser, a FoodShare student nutrition manager, started an innovative "grab and go" fruit stand in the lobby of her son's school in the old City of York, C.R. Marchant Middle School, and later a snack program there. Susan Butler, a former high school teacher who played a pivotal role in the Scarborough Hunger Coalition during her years at FoodShare, helped to start many student nutrition programs city wide. She explained the cake's roots in the First World War, when a shortage of eggs and dairy necessitated baking without these standard ingredients and it was called Whacky Cake.

1½ cups all-purpose flour

1 cup granulated sugar

¼ cup cocoa powder

1 tsp baking soda

½ tsp salt

⅓ cup vegetable oil

1 tsp vanilla extract

1 tsp white vinegar

1 cup grated beets

Preheat oven to 350°F (180°C). Lightly grease a 9- × 5-inch (2.5 L) loaf pan or 13- × 9-inch (3.5 L) cake pan.

In small bowl, sift together flour, sugar, cocoa, baking soda, and salt.

In large bowl, mix oil, vanilla, vinegar, beets, and 1 cup water. Add dry ingredients and stir until combined. Pour into prepared pan. Bake in centre of oven for 40 to 45 minutes or until a toothpick inserted into the centre comes out clean.

Makes 8 servings.

Honey Cake

Contributed by David Garcelon, local food leader and former executive chef of the Fairmont Royal York Hotel, the first hotel in the world to install rooftop beehives. The bees in those hives originated with FoodShare, and continue to be supported through FoodShare's partnership with the Toronto Beekeepers Co-operative, which also tends hives at Downsview Park and the Toronto Botanical Garden and is dedicated to reminding urban dwellers of the importance of pollinators in the food system.

There are many versions of this traditional recipe in circulation. Some use the flesh of the lemon and orange; the Royal York uses the grated rind and juice, and, of course makes the recipe their own by incorporating the raw honey from their hives. Often served at Rosh Hashanah, the cake tastes even better the day after it is made.

½ cup vegetable oil

1 cup granulated sugar

3 eggs, separated

1 cup raw liquid honey

1 apple, cored, peeled, shredded

1 cup raisins

3 cups all-purpose flour

1 tbsp baking powder

1 tsp baking soda

¼ cup whisky, brandy, or apple juice

Finely grated rind and juice of 1 lemon

Finely grated rind and juice of 1 orange

½ cup chopped walnuts

Preheat oven to 325°F (160°C). Grease 13- × 9-inch (3.5 L) metal cake pan.

In large bowl and using electric mixer, beat oil, sugar, and egg yolks until well mixed. Using wooden spoon, stir in honey and apple.

In small bowl, combine raisins with ½ cup flour; stir into batter.

Into another bowl, sift remaining flour with baking powder and baking soda. In two additions, stir into batter. Stir in whisky, lemon and orange rind and juice, and walnuts.

In another bowl and using clean beaters, beat egg whites until stiff. Stir one-quarter into batter, then fold in remaining beaten egg whites. Pour batter into prepared pan.

Bake in centre of oven for 50 to 55 minutes or until tester inserted in centre comes out clean. Cool in pan on rack. Cut into squares.

Makes about 24 servings.

Pastel de Tres Leches

This spongy cake oozing a sweet milk syrup comes from food and travel writer Mary Luz Mejia. A Latin American favourite, its name means "three milk cake." Mary Luz tells us that although she first tried the cake at a birthday party in Miami, "theories abound as to how it was first introduced. Some claim the cake's origins began in Mexico, while others argue that it was perfected in Nicaragua and later adopted by Cuba." FoodShare's financial manager—and longest-serving employee—Gloria Padilla, from Nicaragua, also claims this cake as a family favourite. Use any leftover sweetened condensed milk in coffee.

Cake

5 large eggs, separated
¾ cup granulated sugar
⅓ cup milk
½ tsp vanilla extract
1 cup all-purpose flour
1½ tsp baking powder
½ tsp cream of tartar
¼ cup granulated sugar

Milk Syrup

1½ cups evaporated milk
1 cup sweetened condensed milk
1 cup whipping cream
1 tbsp dark rum (optional)
1 tsp vanilla extract

Preheat oven to 350°F (180°C). Generously butter 13- × 9-inch (3.5 L) cake pan.

For cake, in bowl and using electric mixer, beat egg yolks with ¾ cup sugar until light and thickened, about 5 minutes. Fold in milk, vanilla, flour, and baking powder.

In another bowl and using clean beaters, beat egg whites until foamy. Add cream of tartar; beat until soft peaks form. Gradually add ¼ cup sugar, beating until stiff, glossy peaks form. Gently fold into yolk mixture. Pour into prepared baking dish, smoothing with spatula.

Bake in centre of oven until firm to the touch and toothpick inserted in centre comes out clean, about 30 to 40 minutes. Cool to room temperature.

For milk syrup, in bowl, whisk together evaporated milk, condensed milk, whipping cream, rum (if using), and vanilla. Pierce cake all over with a fork, being careful not to tear it. Pour milk syrup over the cake evenly, including into the corners and along the edges. Let stand until cake absorbs syrup.

If desired, serve pieces of cake with whipped cream, or dust with cocoa powder and serve with sliced mango or other tropical fruit. Store leftovers in the fridge.

Makes about 10 servings.

About FoodShare Toronto

FoodShare partners with community leaders, organizations, and schools in Toronto to increase access to and knowledge of sustainably produced good healthy food. As social entrepreneurs, we root our work in innovation, operational excellence, and fiscal sustainability. As social justice advocates, we prioritize working with underserved communities, sharing tools and expertise to build a just food system.

PROGRAMS

Student Nutrition 🍎 Field to Table Schools 🍎 Good Food Café
Focus on Food youth internships 🍎 Good Food Box
Good Food Markets 🍎 Fresh Produce for Schools and Community Agencies
Baby and Toddler Nutrition 🍎 Community Kitchens
Field to Table Catering 🍎 FoodLink hotline 🍎 Power Soups
Community Gardening 🍎 Composting 🍎 Beekeeping
Urban Agriculture 🍎 Sunshine and Bendale Market Gardens

OUR VISION: GOOD HEALTHY FOOD FOR ALL

FoodShare Toronto (www.foodshare.net) is an innovative non-profit community food organization whose programs include direct fresh produce access, childhood nutrition and education, community cooking, community growing, and urban agriculture. FoodShare improves healthy food access for more than 145,000 children and adults every month across the City of Toronto, and shares food skills and resources with many more in Toronto and across Canada.

Founded in 1985 to address hunger, FoodShare takes a unique multifaceted and long-term approach to hunger and food issues. We work to empower individuals, families, and communities through food-based initiatives, while at the same time advocating for the broader public policies needed to ensure that everyone has adequate access to good, healthy, sustainably produced food. Working "from field to table," we focus on the entire system that puts food on our tables: from the growing, processing, and distribution of food to its purchase, cooking, and consumption.

FoodShare Toronto is a leading Canadian community food security organization, recognized as an important innovator of effective programs that have been reproduced all across the country. We work from the ground up, cultivating awareness, building citizenship, and enhancing individual and community participation, all the while striving to improve access to good healthy food.

FoodShare is a pioneer, creating empowering tools and scalable solutions, taking an open-source approach and sharing those resources freely. Our staff support and mentor communities to draw on their own strengths in order to develop and tailor solutions. This community development partnership model means that our work is leveraged exponentially as information and skills are adapted and passed along to others, ensuring that each dollar we invest in our programs multiplies and affects the greatest possible number of people by providing tools and support that continue giving.

OUR APPROACH

- **Long-term vision for ending hunger** from all angles, working from field to table to empower people through Canada's most successful non-profit food hub, which connects urban dwellers directly to fresh produce, to local farmers, to each other, and to the cooking and growing skills needed to choose healthy food for a healthy future.
- **Universal programs** to help everyone overcome hurdles to saying yes to healthy food and removing the stigma for those who will benefit most deeply.
- **Community development partnership model** that supports communities with information and tools (so they don't have to reinvent the wheel), honours neighbourhood leadership and strength, and creates long-term solutions with ever-increasing impact.
- **Sustainable social enterprise programs** to pay farmers fairly while making quality produce and home-cooked meals accessible to all through subsidized food distribution models, the Field to Table Community Food Hub, and Field to Table Catering.

Join us in putting food first to build healthy communities. Together, we will make Good Healthy Food for All a reality!

VISIT

All are welcome to visit FoodShare's exciting non-profit Field to Table Community Food Hub at 90 Croatia Street, Toronto, Ontario, M6H 1K9 to share the hope that inspires us every day and see your support at work. Please call 416.363.6441 to arrange your tour.

You can also find all our resources and tools, plus our bustling hub of community food activity, online at www.foodshare.net.

SUPPORT

Warmest thanks to all who support FoodShare: our visionary donors; core funders United Way Toronto and the City of Toronto; and all the foundations, faith groups, unions, and levels of government that—in combination with hundreds of volunteers, staff, and community partners—have helped us to make a difference in the lives of millions.

With your help, FoodShare has become a leading Canadian community food security organization. By sharing with us, you have helped develop important innovations, making an impact community by community as skills and resources are passed along to many more.

If you would like to make a donation or find out more about how to help, please visit **www.foodshare.net** or call us.

Index

ADRIENNE DE FRANCESCO (left) is a creative home cook who knows
FoodShare inside out. She delights in exploring and sharing all
things food: where it comes from and how to grow it, to the many
ways in which it feeds us all, body and soul.

MARION KANE (right) has been a leader in the world of food writing
for more than 30 years and has authored three cookbooks. She
was food editor/columnist for Canada's largest newspaper, the
Toronto Star, for 18 years and is now a freelance food sleuth, writer,
broadcaster, and cook.